Making Supervision
Work for You

Education at SAGE

SAGE is a leading international publisher of journals, books, and electronic media for academic, educational, and professional markets.

Our education publishing includes:

- accessible and comprehensive texts for aspiring education professionals and practitioners looking to further their careers through continuing professional development

- inspirational advice and guidance for the classroom

- authoritative state of the art reference from the leading authors in the field

Find out more at: **www.sagepub.co.uk/education**

Making Supervision Work for You

A Student's Guide

Jerry Wellington

Los Angeles | London | New Delhi
Singapore | Washington DC

© Jerry Wellington 2010

First published 2010

Apart from any fair dealing for the purposes of research
or private study, or criticism or review, as permitted
under the Copyright, Designs and Patents Act, 1988, this
publication may be reproduced, stored or transmitted in
any form, or by any means, only with the prior
permission in writing of the publishers, or in the case
of reprographic reproduction, in accordance with the
terms of licences issued by the Copyright Licensing
Agency. Enquiries concerning reproduction outside
those terms should be sent to the publishers.

SAGE Publications Ltd
1 Oliver's Yard
55 City Road
London EC1Y 1SP

SAGE Publications Inc.
2455 Teller Road
Thousand Oaks, California 91320

SAGE Publications India Pvt Ltd
B 1/I 1 Mohan Cooperative Industrial Area
Mathura Road
New Delhi 110 044

SAGE Publications Asia-Pacific Pte Ltd
33 Pekin Street #02-01
Far East Square
Singapore 048763

Library of Congress Control Number: 2009931937

British Library Cataloguing in Publication data

A catalogue record for this book is available from
the British Library

ISBN 978-1-84860-617-3
ISBN 978-1-84860-618-0 (pbk)

Typeset by C&M Digitals (P) Ltd, Chennai, India
Printed in India at Replika Press Pvt Ltd
Printed on paper from sustainable resources

Contents

About the author

Jerry Wellington is a professor and head of research degrees in the School of Education at the University of Sheffield. He has supervised a large number of PhD and professional doctorate students and has been external examiner for a wide range of doctoral theses at universities in the UK and overseas. Currently, his main interests are in research methods and in postgraduate education. He has written many journal articles and books on education, methods and methodology, and the role of new technology in education.

Acknowledgements

I would like to thank:

- All of the supervisors and students whom I interviewed and agreed to keep anonymous.
- The students and staff I interviewed for the Virtual Graduate School, produced by the University of Sheffield. These interviews influenced and shaped my own views on the viva and the nature of a 'good thesis' in ways which are hard to make explicit and fully acknowledge.
- Professor Pam Denicolo of the University of Reading for allowing me to reproduce her valuable list of attributes for a good thesis in Chapter 9.
- Everyone who read earlier drafts of the chapters in this book and gave valuable formative feedback, especially Marianne Lagrange, Pam Denicolo, Jason Sparks and Matthew Waters.

Introduction

The aim of this book is to take a close look at the supervision process from start to finish. There are other books on supervision but I hope that this one offers new perspectives on supervision, bringing in both the student's and the supervisor's points of view.

Some of the questions the book addresses are:

- Who is supervision important for ... and why?
- What ground rules need to be negotiated at the start?
- What are the delicate checks and balances needed in a successful supervision relationship?
- What phases are there in the supervision journey?
- Which ways of workings can facilitate progress on this journey and what are some of the barriers?
- What are the vitally important interactions in the supervision process, whether face to face, online or both?
- What could – and should – supervisors and students expect from each other when it comes to the business of writing?
- How should examiners be chosen ... and who by?
- What are the key criteria for a 'good thesis'? What do examiners actually look for?
- What is meant by 'originality'?
- How can students, with their supervisors, prepare and be prepared for the viva?
- After the viva, is there a role for your supervisor? Why publish your work ... and what puts people off?

The book has been written primarily for students from any part of the world, but it is also intended to be of value to supervisors, new or experienced.

The book includes a range of voices on the supervision process, from both students and supervisors. These are included at various points in the book, especially in the earlier chapters. I am not pretending that they are representative or generalisable in any way (is there such a thing as generalisability?);

but I can say that these were views actually expressed to me in face to-face-interviews, audio-recorded, transcribed my me and sent back to the intervie-wees for their approval.

This book is based on a range of foundations. Firstly, my writing is based on my own experiences as a student, a supervisor, an internal examiner and an external examiner. I have lost count of the number of vivas I have been part of, but I estimate that the number is approaching a hundred. Secondly, the book is based on my own research and studies of the literature over the last twenty years or more – some of these sources are listed in the References and suggested in the Further Reading sections at the end of each chapter. Finally, the book has been influenced by the excellent interviews I mentioned above. I am very grateful to all who gave up their time to have those dialogues with me.

I hope that the book is interesting, thought-provoking and useful to those who read it. If you have any criticisms, praise, suggestions or comments on its chapters please direct them to me at: j.wellington@sheffield.ac.uk.

1

Opening up the supervision process

Chapter aims

This chapter begins to open up and examine the process of supervision by discussing:

- whether supervision is important;
- who is involved in the process;
- who supervision is important for ... and why;
- whether supervision is a form of teaching;
- different ways of describing the supervision process.

In different sections we draw on the views of a range of supervisors and students.

Is supervision important?

Of course, my own answer is yes – otherwise I would not be writing this book. What about the views of others? A book chapter by Hill et al., back in 1994, highlighted several claims made prior to that time by different authors:

- Supervision is 'crucial' (Burnett, 1977: 17; Phillips and Pugh, 1987: 22).
- Supervision is 'pivotal' (Council of Graduate Schools, 1991: 22).
- Supervision is 'at the core of the project' (Connell, 1985: 41).
- Supervision is the 'single most important variable affecting the success of the research project' (ESRC, 1991: 8).

Most supervisors, and students who have recently completed their theses, would agree with the sentiments behind these claims: supervisors are a vitally important part of the student's development and journey. The purpose of this book is to discuss the role of the supervisor and how students can best work with their supervisors in achieving their aims. We start from the premise that making the most of the supervision process is a joint responsibility, requiring equal commitment from both parties – the onus is a shared one.

Others are involved too ...

Increasingly supervisors are not the only key element. The changing context of supervision, which we look at in more detail in Chapter 2, has brought about at least two changes which directly affect the supervision process and the relationship it entails. Firstly, the relationship is not quite the cosy, behind-closed-doors experience that perhaps it once was. In many cases it is not just a case of 'the student and supervisor' going it alone. One change has been the increase in co-supervision in many university departments which means that the process may involve three people (or even more in some cases I have come across) rather than the traditional two. (I have heard this described as a *ménage à trois* rather than a *folie à deux*).

In addition, students in most universities are signing up for a programme now rather than a supervisor or supervisors – this programme, whether a student is on a professional doctorate or a PhD, may well involve research training (often accredited), residential weekends, study schools, a peer seminar programme and events laid on by the Graduate School, doctoral centre or similar organisation. The doctoral journey has shifted from being likened to the apprenticeship years (with the novice and his master, to use the gendered language of the early days of apprenticeships) more towards a community of practice, in which the student gradually plays a more central part in the community after starting at the periphery. Both these ideas relate to the notion of 'legitimate peripheral participation' by the student (Hasrati, 2005) which we discuss and question later. Perhaps the most tangible or visible difference in the current context (compared to the 1990s from which the above bullet points were taken) is that there are now taught elements in the doctorate, programmes of training (even though that term is not to everyone's liking), a new skills agenda, greater possibilities for peer networking (either face to face or electronically), and new possibilities for collaboration and feeling part of a cohort or a community. In short, the supervisor is no longer the single pivot or crux on which the doctorate hinges (to mix a few metaphors). Isolation and 'cosiness' are to some extent things of the past now, although as we see in later chapters they still need to be guarded against.

Who is supervision important for?

Most students view the process of being supervised as very important for them. As one of the students I interviewed put it:

> I think it is important for me – I know from my own experience that after I've met with Jane [pseudonym] I'm really productive for the first few weeks after that. And in the days just before I meet her again I find myself a bit adrift again … and then we meet and then I'm back on track. We e-mail a lot, almost every day, but it's not the same as actually meeting face to face. And I don't know what she does because she seems to have such a light touch … but somehow she kind of gets me back on track. I'm puzzled often about what she does; I think she just asks a few, very pertinent, questions?

This student and others I have interviewed commonly use the notion of being 'off and on track':

> When I'm 'off track' my thinking seems to wander about all over the place, and I can't seem to focus and go in a certain direction. I can't seem to alight on anything that takes me forward. And that stops after I've met Jane again. I stop wandering about. Very recently I think I do know where my track is going now [after 18 months of her PhD]. My supervisor kept reassuring me that this would happen and that really helped.

> I think it's really important. It keeps you on track. It's good to have a time frame and to know that the supervisor will read your work and give you feedback. I can't imagine doing it without supervision. Moving from a taught course to a PhD is a complete change – going from lots of contact hours to very few. Supervision is necessary at regular intervals to ensure that the student is on track and hasn't taken too big a diversion from the question.

We also need to recognise that supervision is important for two other parties involved: the supervisor her or himself and the organisation they work for. Firstly, for supervisors themselves, the rewards may be intrinsic and extrinsic: the process is often a learning experience, a way of helping to keep up to date, sometimes a career development move, and for many a source of personal satisfaction. Equally, the presence of research degree students can provide kudos or status not only to a university lecturer but also to the department or the organisation as a whole. For example, in the research assessment exercises of the past, the presence of a critical mass of research degree students in a department has contributed to the grading of their research culture and environment and ultimately to the income they received.

Some of the supervisors I interviewed expressed their personal views on the importance of supervision:

3

I see it [supervision] as being essential in terms of the student, but I also see it as important for me, in keeping my currency in the field; and I think it's important for the University, especially the one I am at here, where the research culture has not traditionally been strong.

I learn an awful lot from my students because they inevitably introduce me to work and reading that I might not have come across from my own bat. But as well as that, some of the people I have supervised have become very good friends ... there is also a lot of satisfaction to do with helping some-body, not only with their academic life sometimes.

I think it's very important for both student and supervisor. It's important for me as an academic because it allows me to learn about parts of my own field that I don't necessarily know that well. But even in a field I do know well they will teach me things because they will take a different line of enquiry, they will often take an interesting methodological approach that I might not know that much about ... and sometimes they will take a con-ceptual approach that has a lot to teach me. In terms of the student, it depends on the student and they vary hugely, for two reasons. One is that they need to know the rules of the game. They can set off with some pretty free-floating ideas and they have to be reined in – also, ultimately, they have to produce a thesis which can be examined. And I know, having exter-nally examined a lot of theses now, you can tell immediately how good the supervision has been.

Students should remind themselves of all the above points if ever they have feelings of being a burden on their supervisor or being demanding (as I have heard some supervisors describe certain students). Equally, I have heard supervisors tell their student how busy they are: yes, but supervision is part of the job, they are paid for it, it counts towards their workload and it brings recognition and income. It is not voluntary work.

Opening up the supervision process

There has been a history of seeing supervision as something that takes place behind closed doors, between consenting adults – a 'secret garden' to use the popular cliché. As Pearson and Brew (2002: 138) put it, there has been a tradition of seeing supervision 'as a set of implicit and unexamined processes'. Similarly, Johnson et al. (2000: 135) suggested that 'Post graduate supervision – and more generally the pedagogic practices of the PhD – have largely remained unscrutinised and unquestioned.' There has been an assumption that if you can do research then you can supervise it, or if you have been supervised yourself to doctoral level then you know how to be a supervisor. This is about as valid an assumption as the belief that good footballers make good football managers (or the equivalent assumption in any sport or area of activity).

This has changed in recent years – and certainly since those articles were written – with the advent of a range of documents outlining the principles of and precepts for supervision, as well as the many publications which we consider in this book which discuss and sometimes theorise the supervision process. The supervision process is now beginning to receive the study and scrutiny that teaching and learning have received over the last century and before. In this book we consider what sort of a process supervision is and how one can make the most of it.

The word 'supervision' is in common use, certainly in the UK, but in some ways it has certain, perhaps unwanted, connotations. In many places the term 'adviser' is preferred. The verb 'to supervise' is related in most dictionaries to the verbs to oversee, to survey and to inspect. The noun 'supervisor' is sometimes defined as a person who 'exercises general direction or control over a business or a body of workmen' or as one 'who inspects and directs the work of others' (*Shorter OED*).

Many students and their supervisors would be very uncomfortable with the language of controlling, surveying, overseeing and inspecting. Some would be more at ease with the idea of 'directing', but we will see in later chapters that a delicate balance needs to be maintained between being left alone and being directed.

The varied comments from students and staff whom I interviewed for this book indicate a wealth of views on the supervision process and its importance. A range of descriptors and metaphors for the supervisor are used to express what the process means to individuals: a sounding board, a mirror, an anchor, a torch (leading the way, showing you where to go), a guide, a mentor …

Supervisors' views included:

I see myself as a critical friend – I am some people's mummy too, but not everybody's.

I respond rather than supervise.

I'm a bit like a tennis coach – you work on different aspects, it's one to one, you've got to help them with style, and they have to compete at the end – well, 'perform' anyway, in the viva.

A student I interviewed described her supervisor as:

Like an anchor … if I'm kind of like a ship, sometimes I can be sailing along quite smoothly, other times I'm in rough seas and I just need to drop the anchor, just to stay still for a bit. And I'm kind of in control: I can decide when to pull the anchor up, or decide when to drop it down. It's that real steadying influence that Jane provides. I can get a bit excitable and Jane always calms me down – it's not good to be that excited because then I don't think critically enough.

In summary, people draw upon a variety of metaphors and images when they reflect upon the supervision process. One of the main themes of this book is that no one metaphor, theory or model will fit the activity of supervising or being supervised. Every student–supervisor relationship is different. There is no one template, framework or style of supervision that can be relied upon in guiding supervision or in training people to do it. No one style or format will fit all. One of the supervisors I interviewed sums this up neatly by saying:

When I take someone on I always ask them what they want from me. Everybody is an individual ... and everybody interacts differently with me.

Is supervision a form of teaching?

Many discussions have suggested that supervision is a form of teaching (for example Connell, 1985). Brown and Atkins go further (1988: 115) by arguing that 'research supervision is probably the most *complex and subtle* form of teaching in which we engage'. Writing from a supervisor's perspective I would tend to agree. Supervision is a form of teaching and my own experience is that it requires subtlety, tact, patience, understanding and rapport. In short, it involves both the cognitive domain and the affective (which we discuss fully later). However, many teachers would argue that teaching of any kind and at any level is complex and subtle and is premised on the same requirements as I have listed above. Perhaps the big difference is that supervision of a research degree involves several factors that may not be present in teaching at (say) secondary school level, college or university.

Firstly, it requires the development of a long-term working relationship (some would also argue that the relationship is to an extent a personal one too; in reality, the two are often linked). This is probably more complex and subtle than a one-off lecture or even a lecture programme for a group of 100 undergraduates; certainly and obviously, the supervision of a research degree is a far longer-term experience, especially for part-time students.

Secondly, and unfortunately in my view, the dominant metaphor for teaching at many levels is that of 'delivering': a metaphor that I often call the Postman Pat model of pedagogy. The word 'delivery' is now so prevalent in meetings and committees that it has become hard to avoid. It implies a transmission model of teaching: the expert teacher is conveying a commodity called knowledge to the students who lack this commodity (often compared with filling a tank with petrol).

But the supervision of a research degree can never be a matter of delivery. As some of my supervisor interviewees put it:

> I see it as a developmental role with the individual, not a transactional role ... it's more intimate, and it's a more direct communication with the individual learner. It's much more a developmental relationship with a peer, or a near peer, rather than with a student in a more subordinated role. That's important because the person who will be the expert in the student's field will be the student, not me. In other teaching, I approach the students as to some extent in deficit that they need some discrete knowledge that is transferred to them.

> I think it is a form of teaching because you are kind of guiding somebody through the literature and helping them shape their ideas ... it's different because they have potentially quite a bit more freedom to shape things than, say, a student writing an assignment. The other difference is that, although you learn a lot in any teaching, in PhD supervision you learn a lot more from them. The one-to-one relationship is obviously different to your main teaching and the chance to get to know somebody over three or four years or whatever is much greater. You do have to start with where the students are and their interests ... but having said that you also have to display your expertise. There are things that supervisors know but students don't and that's where there is a kind of formal teaching side to it, in any supervision.

> I suppose I don't think of supervision as 'teaching'. But in the sense of my own reflection on what's happened during a supervision session, and how things worked or didn't, and what I've learnt from it and what I would and wouldn't do again then it is a form of teaching. But the power relationship is different to teaching in a classroom – in supervision I don't think of it in that way, or I try not to, because in many instances the students know a great deal more about what they're doing than I do. I see it more as a 'mirror' in a sense where sometimes your role is to reflect, to bounce questions back at them, to be a critical friend – to ask 'what is it you really mean here?' One of the things I ask them to do is to see me as their critical reader. I see my role as being that critical reader and saying 'you've not convinced me yet'.

In most situations, the supervision process involves guiding a student through something of a personal journey. Thus the dominant metaphors for supervision are likely to relate to guidance, companionship (even friendship), navigation, direction and motivation rather than transmission or delivery. A student who enters a supervisory relationship with the latter two models (transmission and delivery) dominating their expectations is likely to be disappointed. Equally, the extent to which the other metaphors are taken literally in the supervisory relationship needs to be reflected upon and we return to this later in the book. For example, to what extent should the supervisor be a 'director'? Or even a 'navigator'? One supervisor I interviewed describes his role as:

> ... a companion, with them on their doctoral journey. So my job is to be sup-portive, to be open, to be there, to be present. I've never set out to be a 'friend' but I do try to be someone they can rely on and trust – and equally to be honest, as you would expect a friend to be.

In conclusion ...

Supervision and a student's relationship with her or his supervisor are vitally important for success at postgraduate level. But there are other important elements in the journey: peer networks, ICT and library support, critical friends, other academic and administrative staff in the department, the presence of a community of practice and the cohort effect in many professional doctorates. We discuss these in different chapters throughout the book.

Supervision can be seen as a form of teaching, and is complex and subtle. But it differs from other models and modes of teaching at different levels of education and is often described using a variety of different metaphors. No one metaphor or model of supervision will fit all situations. The key features of good supervision in the current context are adaptability and flexibility.

 Further reading

Eley, A. and Jennings, R. (2005) *Effective Postgraduate Supervision*. Maidenhead: Open University Press.

Johnson, L., Lee, A. and Green, B. (2000) 'The PhD and the autonomous self', *Studies in Higher Education*, 25 (2), 135–47.

Leonard, D. (2001) *A Woman's Guide to Doctoral Studies*. Buckingham: Open University Press.

2

The changing context for postgraduate supervision ... and why it matters

Chapter aims

This chapter starts with a brief history of the doctorate. We go on to consider:

- shifts in the climate surrounding – and the control of – the supervision process;
- discussions and criticisms about the nature of the doctorate and what it is 'for';
- the changing context for postgraduate study and how this affects current practice;
- the dimensions of change at a variety of levels, from global down to institutional.

Why consider these changes and the evolving context? Why does this matter to individual students? The short answer is that the background is highly relevant for later sections and chapters when we consider what a doctorate is, how it is examined, what happens in the viva and what supervision is or should be.

A historical perspective on the idea of a 'doctorate'

The concept of a doctorate has always been clear. As the highest degree that can be awarded it proclaims that the recipient is worthy of being listened to *as an equal* by the appropriate university faculty. (Phillips and Pugh, 2000: 20)

The same authors also write that a 'doctor's degree is a licence to teach', as compared with a master's degree which is a 'licence to practise'. They also suggest that to acquire a doctorate is to become a 'fully professional researcher' (p. 21). My own view is that the concept of 'doctorateness' is far from clear in the current era (see Chapter 5 for a full discussion).

For now, let us focus on the word 'doctor', which is an interesting one. Its original meaning is that of a teacher or instructor, being derived from the Latin 'docere' (to teach). Similarly, the word 'docile' means, literally, 'teachable', though it is rarely used in that sense now. The closely related term, to educate, is also derived from Latin, in this case 'educere' (to lead forth). Taylor and Beasley (2005: 7) also refer to the original concept of the doctorate, going back to the twelfth century, as being primarily a licence to teach in a certain subject area. But they argue that 'modern' doctoral degrees can be traced back to the early nineteenth century and the introduction of the PhD in Berlin by their progenitor, Von Humboldt, whose intention was to improve the supply of scientists and other researchers by allowing them to undertake a 'solo research project' under the guidance of a senior professor or *Doktorvater*. Thus the main elements of this conception of the doctorate involved a guided research topic in which the student gradually became an expert and would make an independent contribution to knowledge in that chosen field, a written dissertation submitted for examination, followed by an oral defence.

In some ways this contrasts sharply with the American model: the first PhD in the US was awarded by Yale in 1861; Harvard, Michigan and Pennsylvania followed (Taylor and Beasley, 2005: 8). The model adopted there involved a formal stage of course work of two or three years, an interim period involving other requirements including some teaching, followed by a general examination and then finally research and writing for a dissertation, culminating in a 'defence' (a word we return to later).

In many ways, these contrasting models of the doctorate can be seen in the current tensions and debates around doctoral programmes of the twenty-first century: between teaching and 'guidance'; between student autonomy and dependence, and similarly between laissez-faire supervision and a high level of direction; between formal writing requirements at earlier stages (as in most professional doctorates) and simply 'writing up' for the dissertation only; and the tension between various 'institutional' demands made on students such as formal, accredited research training or the acquisition of 'generic skills' compared with an idealised model of a doctorate in which the student simply 'gets on with it'. We explore these tensions again in Chapter 4.

Taylor and Beasley (2005: 9) point out that the German PhD, unlike Heineken lager, did not reach other parts of Europe as readily as it had been accepted in the USA. It took until 1920 for the first doctorate (a DPhil at

Oxford) to be awarded in the UK – the other UK universities followed over the next decade (Simpson, 1983). Ironically, although they had taken a century to do it, they largely adopted the German model, i.e. the focus was the student's own research project. This form of PhD was subsequently adopted by other parts of the world such as Australia, with its first doctoral programme in 1946.

By the 1980s and 1990s the doctorate had spread worldwide but had also become criticised on several counts. The context for doctoral study also began to shift during this era.

The move from academic autonomy to the audit culture

Many would say that the UK moved into an age of accountability (and probably other countries too) in the era of Margaret Thatcher, i.e. from 1979. Some have called this change the 'accountability revolution'. Others have called it the advent of the 'audit culture'. Professionals were no longer left to just 'get on with the job' and trusted to do it professionally and effectively. Increasingly, teachers, lecturers, nurses, doctors and many other professionals were scrutinised and checked to see if they were doing the job properly. The management styles and practices of the private business sector were being adopted by universities (see Deem, 1998, who discusses this 'new managerialism') and to some extent schools. Some would argue that this was long overdue, not least in doctoral supervision. Others argued, and still do, that the advent of accountability undermined the autonomy, self-respect and self-esteem of the professional. Gradually, as critics such as Duke (1992) have argued, the 'old discourse' involving terms such as culture, discipline, excellence and scholarship was replaced by the 'new discourse' of efficiency, fitness for purpose, quality, value-added and performance management. My own view, discussed further later, is that in some ways the traditional academic virtues and demands of a doctorate have remained constant, but it cannot be denied that these shifts have radically changed the supervision process – for both students and supervisors.

These shifts can be presented starkly as in Table 2.1, although the reality is much more complex and messy than this. These shifts are, of course, caricatures of the complex changes which have taken place. It should also be pointed out that any feelings of nostalgia for the 'good old days' of autonomy should be tempered by the fact that it could be described using more critical terms such as 'secrecy', 'laissez-faire' or anything goes. In more colloquial language, a critic of past practices might say that supervisors could get away with anything. Whatever one's view of the past (as either the halcyon days or as a time when staff could and did do whatever they wanted to), in terms of

Table 2.1   Moves towards an 'audit culture'

A shift from ...	To ...
Self-regulation	External regulation, prescription
Autonomy	External control and monitoring
Responsibility	Accountability
Trust (implicit)	Checks, guarantees, contracts (explicit)
'Behind closed doors'	Visibility, transparency
A community of scholars	A degree factory

doctoral education, these shifts meant that the whole process was increasingly taken out of its 'secret garden' (to use the cliché) and placed under public scrutiny and the inevitable adjunct of audit and quality control.

Rumblings about the doctorate

We do not have space to go into details here but, because they have had a strong influence on the current supervision process, I summarise the main criticisms that were being made of doctoral education below.

The first rumblings perhaps concerned the low completion rate for doctoral students and the long duration of the process in many cases. Taylor and Beasley (2005: 10) list a number of studies showing that only around half of all doctoral students were actually completing in the era of the 1980s and 1990s. Equally, they cite other studies indicating that far fewer completed within the allotted time, with one study finding that less than one-fifth of sponsored students completed within four years.

The concerns about completion and duration were matched by rumblings about what a doctorate was (and is) actually for. Is it training for academia (like the old licence to teach) or is it a preparation for life outside the academy? If the latter, is it relevant (to use an oft overdone term)? Does it contribute to economic growth or other utilitarian aims? If it does not have utility value what is its intrinsic worth? Is it dealing with the right kind of knowledge – is it producing what has been called 'mode 1 knowledge', i.e. creating knowledge for its own sake with the age-old academic virtues? Or should it now be concerned with 'mode 2 knowledge production', e.g. solving real-life problems, applying knowledge, creating commercial opportunities for knowledge transfer and leading to wider dissemination and exploitation? Similarly, was and is the doctorate too narrow, too specialised and too single-disciplined as opposed to being broad, related to real problems and therefore interdisciplinary?

Thus a range of rumblings and direct criticisms have characterised the debate about doctorates over the last twenty years or more.

Responses to these rumblings

The advent of accountability and quality control (for some, not before time; for others a direct infringement of their academic autonomy and professionalism) has had important effects which impinge upon the supervision process today. People are no longer left to their own devices.

Through evolution, regulation and (in some countries) legislation, not only has the context for the doctorate changed but also more tangible things now happen in most universities. A sizeable component of research training, in many cases compulsory, formal and accredited, is now an element of the doctoral programme. Many universities now have Graduate Schools (the first in the UK being at Warwick in 1989) which provide support for, guidance to and (some would say) control over individual departments. A component of training in generic or key skills, deemed to be important for employability, is now a ubiquitous feature of doctoral programmes (these have been widely criticised and will be discussed later). Direct quality control through bodies such as the QAA (Quality Assurance Agency, 2004) in the UK is now given in concrete terms with the explicit statement of precepts or principles to guide supervisors and students.

Dimensions of change

Alongside these overt and covert criticisms of the doctorate and its purpose, a number of wider contextual changes were occurring which greatly affected the reality of the supervision process.

Changes in students

One of the main changes in recent years has been the sheer numbers of people entering higher education (HEFC, 2005, 2007). This huge growth has often been called 'massification'. The growing number taking undergraduate degrees has inevitably led to a rise in numbers going on to masters' and thence doctoral level. A kind of qualification inflation has taken place. As a result, there has been a rise not only in the volume of participation but also in the width of participation. Taylor and Beasley (2005: 18) describe this as the 'precocious few' becoming the 'diverse many'. My own view is that the sheer rise in numbers has not been matched by an increased 'width' or range in students who now engage in higher education. There has been some broadening of the range of students in terms of ethnicity and social class but (as with undergraduates) the rise in number has not been due to a vast increase in breadth. However, it can be said that there are more female students than there were undertaking research degrees, far more part-time students and far more of a mature age.

Changes in students' aims, aspirations and motivations

The centuries-old concept of the doctorate as a licence to teach may still be an important motivation for some students – in particular those who wish to teach and probably do research in the higher education sector. But there is now a plethora of other reasons and motives for taking on the considerable challenge of a doctoral programme – some may be very new, others may be as long as the history of the doctorate itself.

The first group can be called intrinsic aims and motivations. These might fall into several categories. To take on a doctorate is a personal challenge (the highest qualification that one can reach) and to succeed will be a great source of satisfaction and a huge personal achievement. This may be as much the case for the so-called 'high flyer' as for someone who feels they have something to prove, e.g. if they struggled or even failed at an earlier stage in their education. Equally, the desire to pursue one's own interest or curiosity in an area or field of study is a great driver for many. There may be a wish to continue and take deeper an interest which developed at undergraduate or masters' level – there may even be a more long-standing ambition that a student wishes to fulfil. Here, the desire to make a significant, new contribution to a field of study (one of the criteria for a doctorate, as we discuss later) may well be a very personal goal. These aims and others similar to them might be called intrinsic goals – they are important elements in sustaining the drive and energy needed to complete a doctorate, especially in phases of the journey where doubts start to creep in, as we discuss later. Cryer (2000: 7) even argues that they are 'essential reasons' for doing a research degree and that if a student does not have these reasons, perhaps they 'should think again' about embarking on it.

In contrast, there may be a whole set of extrinsic reasons for taking on the challenge of a research degree. It may be a ticket for a job or for some it may be a way of keeping their job as the ground rules and levels of qualification required change; it may provide career enhancement for those already working (who often take a part-time PhD or a professional doctorate); it may be seen as a natural progression, the thing to do or the next step – a kind of 'finishing school' to complete the collection of qualifications. It may be seen as a way of making parents proud or, more cynically, colleagues envious. For some, the acquisition of the title Doctor or Dr may be an extrinsic aim – it can raise self-esteem. More practically I was told on gaining my own doctorate that the title would help when booking a table at a restaurant – true perhaps, but not of great benefit if a diner on the next table is suddenly taken ill and your name is called.

In short, there is a diversity of reasons for wanting to undertake a research degree, some intrinsic, some extrinsic, though the line between them is faint (see Wellington and Sikes, 2006, for further discussion). Also, they are not mutually exclusive – the same person can have several reasons and motivations at different times in the process, and the individual student may need to draw upon their own reservoir of reasons and motivations at different phases and stages, as we see later. Supervisors can help here.

Change from the supervisor's perspective

As we touched upon in Chapter 1, students and supervisors should remind themselves that supervisors now have a range of motives for their involvement in the process too. As above, some may be intrinsic: the satisfaction of seeing a student achieve; the enjoyment of engaging with someone at the same intellectual level who may go on to be more of an expert in their chosen field than you are; the learning experience that many supervisors comment on. But in the modern university context, the extrinsic gains of supervising are not to be underestimated. Individuals can improve their own reputation and CV by successfully supervising; still on a personal level, they can gain promotion as a result (this is one of the listed criteria in many universities for promotion to senior lecturer or reader). Some staff have used the recruitment and successful supervision of research degree students as one means towards building centres of excellence around themselves. More cynically, other supervisors have used students as their own unpaid research assistants, helping them to further their own research. Others have, more justifiably, worked with their research students to produce joint publications which in turn can enhance a CV. At a departmental level, the presence of a critical mass of active research students has been one criterion for success in the research culture and environment aspects of the research assessment exercises (the RAEs) of the past. More widely, this success can transfer to the university as a whole in raising its status and kudos – and even its place in the league tables which began to proliferate at the start of this century.

In summary, it is important for you to recognise that supervisors have a range of sources of satisfaction – and even direct benefit – from their engagement in your work. Students need to remind themselves of this whenever they have feelings of being a burden or if their supervisor should ever have a sharp intake of breath when they are trying to fix the next meeting in the diary.

Broader contextual changes affecting the doctorate

There have been many changes in the personal motivations and aspirations of both supervisors and students – but these have taken place in an institutional, national and global context which has both influenced these aims and been influenced by them.

Globalisation

The term globalisation is often used to describe trends worldwide. It is a highly contested term (see Beck, 2000) but my own perspective is that globalisation, however we define it, has influenced the way we travel, eat, communicate, learn, think and study. It has brought about a level of interconnectedness which was not present in earlier centuries but ironically was given the label 'wryd' by the Anglo-Saxons (meaning roughly the web of life). It was made real during the week in which I am writing this sentence (October 2008) when the collapse of the banking system in Iceland (a country of less than half a million inhabitants) threatened the pay packets of hundreds of thousands of council workers across the UK. This interconnectedness is also an aspect of chaos theory, which suggests that a small change in one part of the world can be, in a sense, multiplied to have far greater effects in another.

Globalisation is partly a result of the idea that the Earth is a system of interrelated parts that enable us to see it as a living whole (the Gaia hypothesis) and partly due to technological change, most notably in air travel and communication. These changes, as with most aspects of 'progress', have been a double-edged sword: the advantages of global air travel are clear but they inevitably have an impact on the planet; the movement of clothes manufacturing away from areas of higher labour costs have led to lower prices but also the exploitation of 'slave labour' in the so-called 'developing world'.

Globalisation has also had a huge impact on education systems and in particular doctoral programmes worldwide. There are several categories of globalisation which have had a real impact on research and study at doctoral level. Drawing on the work of Beck (2000), I have distinguished three relevant categories:

1 *Informational globalisation*. Global communication systems, not least the Internet, mean that countries or organisations now find it harder to block information as, for example, Soviet Russia was once able to. This is not to say that all information which might be valuable to a research degree on every area is freely available – but certainly access to relevant data has been made easier by this aspect of globalisation.

2 *Economic globalisation.* This was made evident by huge economic changes in 2008–9 as a result of the so-called 'credit crunch', which appeared to be triggered by excessive lending to housebuyers in the USA (the 'sub-prime market') leading to a drastic fall in house prices and highly restricted lending virtually worldwide. Other aspects of this crisis included massive changes in currency exchange rates, with the UK pound suffering markedly as compared with (say) the euro, the US dollar and other currencies in China and South East Asia. Economic globalisation of this kind inevitably has an impact on student choices at doctoral level.

3 *Cultural globalisation.* This is not to deny that many parts of the world have their own unique culture which is one of the features that makes travel and studying in another country so appealing. However, some aspects of 'culture' have diffused globally and this may have an impact on the supervision process and interactions between students and supervisors (Appadurai, 1990, talked of 'cultural flows'). An aspect of this could be called 'linguistic globalisation' whereby many expressions in English (or American English) have spread globally, for good or ill, and these may influence anything from face-to-face interactions through to styles of writing in the dissertation.

One key point for doctoral work which Beck (2000) makes in relation to these aspects of globalisation is to stress the 'new importance of the local'. In other words, as globalisation occurs, the diversity and contrast provided by local contexts is increasingly important – this is true in, say, tourism, entertainment and fashion. The local now has a global context. It is equally true in education. Thus knowledge developed and presented in a thesis may have been generated locally but its importance in global terms needs to be emphasised and made explicit in the written thesis and the viva.

The above are just three aspects of globalisation which may have influenced doctoral study – we could probably also add political, ecological, social, techni-cal, ethical and legal globalisation though the definitions of these terms would be contentious (again, see Beck, 2000). However, we should not pretend that globalisation has removed all or even many barriers to research, student free-dom and the development and dissemination of knowledge. There are numer-ous barriers that people face on a daily basis: they may involve religion, gender, race, local culture, human rights and attitudes; they may be financial, social, legal or ethical. These barriers affect existing doctoral students or would-be students as much as any other group; and globalisation has not removed them.

Many students can take an undergraduate degree in their own country but of necessity must go to the so-called developed countries to progress to a mas-ters or a doctorate, at the high, expensive end of the market. This often results in having to travel back and forth to their own country in order to col-lect data for an empirical study. The provision of programmes which allow students to be home based, with staff from (say) a UK university providing two or three study schools per year and electronic contact and tutoring in between has provided a welcome opportunity for many overseas students, with (usually) lower fees. Alternatively, many universities offer 'remote location' programmes in which (typically) a student can remain in his or her home country and may be required to visit the university perhaps once or twice a year, with regular electronic contact in between. Data from Powell and Green (2005) suggest that in the UK, 45 per cent of research students are from other parts of the world, with figures of 25 per cent in France, 20 per cent in Australia and 14 per cent in the USA. These changes have had a huge impact on the nature of research degree programmes and, of course, the supervision process. For example, supervision now commonly involves more electronic contact, fewer face-to-face meetings, greater potential for isolation in some situations and different needs regarding motivation and the affective domain. We discuss these in more detail in later chapters.

Globalisation (with its two key facets of rapid travel and electronic communication) has also been one of the major factors in increasing the diversity of students mentioned earlier.

National and institutional change

Moving down a geographical level, changes at the national level have had a large impact on the supervision process. The move to accountability has led to a rise in regulation, or, as some would say, control. Supervisors are no longer left to conduct doctoral education 'behind closed doors, remote from other teaching or the world of commerce and industry' (as McWilliam and James, 2002: 17, put it). There are national guidelines for quality which can be checked by reviews or, less politely, 'inspections'.

At the institutional level, the main change has been in the guidance and control of the supervision process through published codes of practice and precepts. These may come from a national body such as the Quality Assurance Agency (QAA, 2004: see their website for current information) but in many cases are reinforced at the institutional level through university guidelines and codes of practice. More practically, they are often made concrete at this level by asking supervisors and students to always maintain records of meetings; in some universities student and supervisor(s) are advised to use a particular form, often online, which is then shared among the participants. Whatever the codes of practice and local regulations, they will have an impact on the nature and business of supervision.

Another major change has been the rise in the diversity of doctorates available, with a range of models and versions of the doctorate and modes of study. There has been a huge growth in part-time doctoral programmes but perhaps the key change has been the rise of the professional doctorate in many areas, for example engineering, business, nursing and education. Professional doctorates tend to have a number of features which mark them off from the traditional PhD. Firstly, the professional doctorate will often have a substantial taught component, prior to the thesis stage (although changes in the PhD in terms of adding more teaching or training and the introduction of 'generic skills' input has led to some convergence here – so it is a misnomer to call the professional doctorate the 'taught doctorate' as some do). As a consequence the dissertation for a professional doctorate is likely to be shorter (e.g. 50,000 words instead of 80,000), largely because a consider-able amount of written work has been assessed prior to the thesis stage. Secondly, they are largely taken by working professionals in the same area as the field of study, e.g. education, business administration. Hence, they tend to be mostly part-time and, most importantly for the supervision process, involve the student in juggling all sorts of balls in the air, to use the cliché. Thirdly, the rationale behind the professional doctorate is that the student's thesis is related to her or his profession in some way and should have an impact on it, either in terms of policy changes or directly on practice. My own experience, over twelve years of supervising professional doctorates, is that this is not always the case. The rhetoric has been that the professional doctorate should directly influence a student's practice or at least their field of practice or policy in it – but there is little empirical evidence to show that this has happened. It is certainly an area that needs to be researched. My personal view is that the experience of doing and succeeding in a professional doctorate has a huge influence on the student's personal development and (often) position but the impact on the profession as a whole has yet to be eval-uated (if indeed it could be).

The rise of different doctorates has, or should have had, knock-on effects on supervision: style, pattern, content and timing. Supervising a part-time pro-fessional doctoral student with a full-time job (and perhaps a family) is nec-essarily a very different and more complex job than the supervision of a full-time PhD student whose main concern in life is achieving a doctorate.

Changing views on pedagogy

Finally, there have been huge changes in the way that (most) staff in higher education view the processes of teaching and learning: pedagogy. At one time, the dominant model may have been that of transmission and delivery – knowledge was seen as a relatively unproblematic commodity which needs to be passed to the students who lack this commodity, i.e. they are in deficit. The aim of teaching, rather like filling a car with petrol, is to make good this deficit. If this was the old model, the more prevalent one in higher education takes a view of the learner as being an active 'constructor' rather than a passive recipient. Students construct knowledge for themselves, albeit often with the help of teachers, based on their previous knowledge and understandings, their preferred modes of learning and their own personal motivations and feelings. Learning is not a passive, value-free, emotionless process; learners are not empty vessels (the *tabula rasa* conception) – a student's learning is determined by a range of factors, many to do with their existing conceptions, knowledge, values and feelings. This view of learning does not mean that teaching and supervision are unimportant – in fact, quite the opposite. The constructivist view implies that the supervisory relationship and the processes involved in it are vital. This relationship and the underlying processes are explored in subsequent chapters.

So ... what has really changed that affects the student?

Some have argued that these changes have transformed 'doctoral education across the globe' (e.g. Taylor and Beasley, 2005: 17). Certainly, the diversity of doctorates and the extent to which they are regulated has altered greatly, as have the make-up of the students, and the attitude of staff to pedagogy and supervision. But in other ways, the long-lasting academic virtues required of doctoral study, and in the written and oral examination of them, have remained unchanged. The traditional standards still hold, as we explore in detail in later chapters. Students are still required to make a 'contribution', to have a thesis in its most literal sense, and to complete a substantial body of writing which is clear and coherent. Many university regulations continue to use terms such as 'publishability' and 'originality' in the criteria they state as requirements for doctoral work. Thus the demands of 'doctorateness' have perhaps evolved less than the context surrounding them. On a more tangible level, if you walked into a supervision session in 2010 would you observe a huge difference between the kinds of activities and interactions going on then as compared with 1980? Thus some supervisors will take the view: *Plus ça change, plus c'est la même chose.* Or, less pretentiously, we could say: change, what change?

I asked the supervisors I interviewed: 'Has the context for doctoral supervision changed? How?' Most agreed that the context has altered. Yes, there has been a drive for consistency and standardisation – but the effort to achieve consistency should never be allowed to stunt the originality that we are striving for, and it will always be the case that standards are discipline dependent. How could we ever create an exact comparison between a PhD in (say) mathematics and one in history or philosophy? It has been said that 'the field takes a view' on what a doctorate is, whether the field is engineering, physics or the arts. The importance of the view from the field looks set to continue.

One supervisor summed up her view of the situation by saying:

> In the past it [supervision] has been something that's done behind closed doors. There is much more standardisation of supervision now in terms of what an **entitlement** is – but it still varies as well because different students need differing amounts and different types of supervision. Some elements are the same – but I feel that I am always learning. The context has changed, things like codes of practice and so on, which are clear in one sense but they are all open to different interpretations.

In conclusion ...

Doctorates are now characterised by:

- diversity not uniformity (an increased number and range of students with a range of ages, motivations, attendance patterns, background, class, location and origins, plus a range of models and versions of the doctorate and modes of study);
- a context of globalisation (e.g. rapid travel and electronic communication; influences and competition from Europe, the USA, South East Asia, Australia);
- regulation – quality control, auditing and accountability (at the national and institutional level);
- growing utilitarianism, i.e. increased concerns about utility and purpose for the knowledge economy, with a demand for the PhD to inculcate generic skills which may increase employability;
- an increasingly different view of what learning, teaching and supervision are.

We have also seen, and will see, that there are many recurring tensions and debates around the doctorate, what it actually is and what it is for. For example:

- Is it primarily to make a contribution to knowledge (students as 'producers of knowledge') ... or a personal journey, a personal project, personal development ... or a 'licence to teach'?
- Is it an individual venture (a personal project) ... or a collaborative effort? (Can all the ideas in a dissertation come from the individual as the source? Is this possible?)
- Are students part of a peer group (a community of practice), a cohort ... or is it an isolated journey?
- Are students (or should they be) autonomous ... or directed (by a supervisor, a sponsor or an employer)? Is this a false dichotomy?
- What is supervision? Is it a form of teaching ... or guidance ... or just 'letting them get on with it'?

- Is its purpose to develop the professional researcher ... or the researching professional?
- Who and what is the doctorate for: the individual, the body of knowledge, industry, employers, the public good ...?
- Should the doctorate be purely research and 'the pursuit of knowledge' ... or should it involve imparting generic skills for all students, e.g. communication, employability? (Do the latter depend on some sort of deficit model in students who lack these skills and need to have them inculcated and imparted?)

All of these tensions underlie the supervision process and the assessment of work at this level, whether oral or written. We consider them all at different points in the book.

 Further reading

Beck, U. (2000) *What Is Globalisation?* Cambridge: Polity Press.

Phillips, E. M. and Pugh, D. S. (2000) *How to get a PhD: A Handbook for Students and Their Supervisors,* 3rd edn. London: Open University Press.

Simpson, R. (1983). *How the PhD Came to Britain.* Guildford: Society for Research into Higher Education.

Taylor, S. and Beasley, N. (2005) *A Handbook for Doctoral Supervisors.* London: RoutledgeFalmer.

Wellington, J. and Sikes, P. (2006), '"A doctorate in a tight compartment": why do students choose a professional doctorate and what impact does it have on their personal and professional lives?' *Studies in Higher Education,* 31 (6): 723–34.

3

Getting started and setting the ground rules

 Chapter aims

This chapter discusses the main issues in setting off on the doctoral journey; for most students it will be a totally new learning experience as this will be the first time they will work closely with the same academic (or academics) over an extended period of time. The chapter:

- summarises the key criteria that are important in choosing a university, department and supervisor... and a research topic;
- examines the elements necessary for a strong research proposal and the criteria by which such proposals are often judged;
- discusses the difficult but vitally important activity, in the early stages of the supervision process, of focusing the investigation and making it 'do-able';
- considers the importance of these early stages in agreeing on 'ground rules' and developing relationships;
- highlights the advantages and sometimes disadvantages of co-supervision;
- stresses the value of becoming part of a wider community during the doctoral journey.

Making the initial choices

This book is based on the premise that most readers will already have made their choice of university, department and potential supervisor, so this section is very brief (fuller discussion on the initial choice can be found in Cryer, 2000:

7–26, and Phillips and Pugh, 2000: 6–18). All these choices are complex and a number of criteria come into play. For example, if a student is lucky enough to have a free, unconstrained choice of which institution they would like to apply for, a number of points need to be considered. For example, a particular university may have an excellent name but the important detail lies in the department that one chooses and specifically which person or persons on the staff might be best placed to supervise your chosen topic. First, you need to weigh up the department, probably from its web pages or its prospectus, to see if there is a research culture or environment which supports postgraduate students and encourages them to be part of that culture. Does it have a postgraduate tutor or head of research degrees who oversees supervision and may be someone to turn to for extra help, pastoral advice or counselling? Is the department used to working with a wide diversity of students, e.g. part-time students, mature professionals, overseas students, students who will need supervising at a distance? Then, in considering potential supervisors, certain academic criteria come into play, such as: What is their record of publications and of research? Have they experience in research degree supervision? Are they still 'research active'? You may be able to find out these things from the institution's and the person's web pages. But equally, more personal criteria are important, and these are always more difficult to ascertain: will their style of supervision suit your way of working? Will they be accessible and able to give time to the supervision? Will they be genuinely interested in your proposed field of study? This is where informal contact, perhaps by phone or face to face or e-mail, can be so valuable. Remember that an acknowledged expert in your field, with a lorry load of publications and a name known worldwide, may not always (or ever) be the ideal supervisor.

The department and the individual supervisor(s) are important, but the wider university context for supporting students needs to be looked into with equal care. The university will probably have a Graduate School or similar set-up; it will offer research training of some kind and a programme for developing students' generic skills (though this is often seen as contentious as we discuss later). Are there possibilities for research degree students to meet together, either socially or more formally? Can students present to their peers, for example at internally organised conferences or seminar programmes? Does the university offer pastoral care and student support that might be of value?

Choosing a research topic

This is never an easy task and the subsequent activity of refining that topic to make it 'do-able' (which we discuss later) is equally hard. In the arts, humanities and social sciences it is probably true that a student has more of a free rein than in engineering or science. A student will often choose a topic that is related to their own individual or professional interests (especially for a professional doctorate), perhaps an area that interested them as an undergraduate or even one that is dear to their heart for more personal, life history or emotional reasons. So to some extent they have greater freedom of choice than, for example, a science student who will have to work within one of the research paradigms of the department and within the constraints of the department's resources, laboratory facilities and equipment. Other students may be sponsored or funded by an employer, their own institution or their government and such sponsors will undoubtedly require a say or probably a larger stake in what goes on. But no student will have complete freedom of choice (unless perhaps they shop around across a large number of universities). They will be dependent on the expertise and interests of the staff who are likely to supervise them and this will involve a lot of important, mutual discussion from both supervisor and student about how the area of study is to be shaped and focused.

Writing a research proposal

One of the earliest, but unfortunately the hardest, tasks is to write a clear research proposal; the difficulties with writing initial proposals are 'well recognised' (Cryer, 2000: 21). To a large extent, students have to do this at a very early stage in order to apply for and be accepted onto a research degree programme. This is especially true for the MPhil/PhD, whereas, in contrast, for many professional doctorates the job of writing a research proposal may be the final written assignment in the 'taught' element. It would be unfair to make one of the admission criteria for a PhD the production of a perfectly formed research proposal, with clearly formulated research questions, stating exactly what is to be done and when, how data are to be collected and analysed, which ethical issues will arise, what the literature base will be, and how the study will make a contribution to knowledge in the field. Those may well be the criteria for a finished dissertation, but real-world research is far too unpredictable and messy for the perfectly polished proposal to be an admission requirement. My view is that the research proposal at the admission stage should show potential or mileage and admit that certain aspects of the study, e.g. gaining access to informants, deciding on the sample, will have to be determined as part of the process.

What should a research proposal contain?

I suggest that the initial proposal should address, at least, the following 12 questions:

1   What is my provisional title?
2   What area/field am I investigating or working in?
3   Why is this topic or area important? Why have I decided to study this?
4   What are my main research questions? Where do or did these 'come' from?
5   What has been done in this area already, i.e. an outline, at least, of the likely literature base?
6   What is the context for the study, e.g. global, national, institutional, personal?
7   What theory/theories/theoretical framework can I draw upon?
8   What is the proposed methodology? Why? And which specific methods are likely to be used? Why these and not others?
9   For an empirical study, how will the sample be determined?
10 What issues are likely to emerge around: (a) access, (b) ethics, in the course of the research?
11 How will data be analysed (whether primary or secondary data)?
12 What timescale, approximately, will I try to follow – and is it humanly possible?

And finally, one probably needs to ask: how many doctorates am I writing? (Incidentally, the answer to this question should be 1.)

Criteria for judging a thesis proposal

The criteria below are based on my own experiences of looking at thesis proposals and also on comments made by different markers at different universities. The criteria have been grouped fairly arbitrarily into categories. Clearly these categories link and overlap. The criteria are biased towards empirical studies, i.e. where the student is going to do some fieldwork! Many of the terms will need unpacking or operationalising for new students in order to give them meaning, e.g. 'critical engagement', 'appropriate methodology'.

My experience is that proposals are often said to be good or strong if they have most of the characteristics shown under the following five categories.

1   *Focus*
    – The research questions (RQs) are clearly spelled out and focused

2   *Methodology*
    – Appropriate methodology
    – Very do-able
    – Access has been considered
    – Ethical issues have been considered
    – Examples of potential interview or questionnaire questions have been included
    – Some indication of how the data are to be analysed has been given

3 *Summary of the literature base*
   - The proposed study is located in existing literature and is set in its histori-
     cal and methodological context
   - Detailed, well reviewed
   - Shows 'critical engagement' and understanding of the salient issues
   - Provides a comprehensive literature base
   - Critical reflection on the policy context

4 *Theoretical framework/conceptual clarification*
   - Shows theoretical clarity
   - RQs located within a theoretical framework

5 *General*
   - Has the potential to make an original contribution to the field
   - Generally it has: potential/mileage/currency/scope ...

My experience is that proposals are often said to be 'less good' or 'needing more work' if they show some of the features indicated under the following four categories:

1 *Focus*
   - RQs not clear or are too general
   - RQs just cannot be answered
   - Aims are: too ambitious/too wide ranging/over-optimistic

2 *Methodology*
   - Not clear what will actually be done or why
   - Just cannot be done
   - Not convincing
   - Lacks fine detail/contains little detail/is lacking in detail
   - No triangulation
   - Design not clear
   - Not clear how the methods will actually be applied to this particular
     investigation

3 *Summary of the literature base*
   - Too descriptive (mostly 'reportage'), lacking in criticality

4 *Theoretical framework/conceptual clarification*
   - Largely absent
   - Key terms not defined, clarified or categorised
   - Research design insufficiently focused (cf. category 1)
   - Lack of theoretical clarity

Advice and comments to students at this stage are commonly of the ilk: 'The student will need to work carefully with the supervisor in the early stages on: x, y or z (often research design and planning)'.

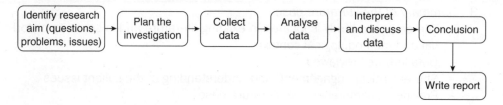

Figure 3.1   Linear traditional idealised approach

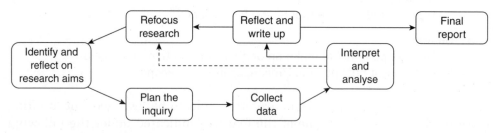

Figure 3.2   Cyclical/realistic

Focusing the research, making it do-able

No research proposal can be perfectly polished or focused at the outset. Indeed, the main purpose of the early stages of supervision is for the student to work with his or her supervisor on achieving more focus, improving the research design and, not least, making it do-able. This is a large job and will take time – in many cases, a clearer focus may not even emerge until after the student has started empirical work and begun to see what can or cannot be done in 'the field'. It is a constant process of thinking, refining, going back, checking and sometimes guessing. As the Nobel prize-winning scientist Sir Peter Medawar described it, scientific method is a 'mixture of guesswork and checkwork' (Medawar, 1963 and 1976).

Thus the research process is not a linear one, as in Figure 3.1, but is cyclical or iterative, as in Figure 3.2.

The early stages

Induction and socialisation

Very few postgraduates will have the same level and intensity of induction as most undergraduates when they first enter university. This may be seen as a blessing by those who remember or witness each year the activities and experiences of 'Freshers' Week', 'Intro Week' or whatever it may be called. However, many universities do offer induction events and programmes for masters and doctoral students and these can be very valuable. For other postgraduate students though, the fact that they may start a course (usually an MPhil or a PhD) at any time of the year makes the feeling of being part of a group induction or initiation hard to achieve. By contrast, in many professional doctorates the whole group begins as a cohort and induction into the computing system, library, ways of working and so on can be easier and certainly create a feeling of being part of a peer network (what is often called the 'cohort effect').

Getting started

Whatever the induction offered, students should take advantage of it. Many postgraduate students are returning to higher education after a long break and, as one of my mature part-time students put it at our first meeting, 'it's a long time since I wrote a thousand words.' A good way of getting started and being 'inducted' is to make a small start with a short, achievable piece of writing, with a mutually agreed deadline. It might be 1,000 words discussing a journal article, for example. This can be shared, in a friendly context, with the supervisor(s) – it can then form the focus of an early discussion. This not only gives a feel of having started but also gives the student (and supervisor) an early feel for the process of doctoral work (and longer term, of getting published: see Wellington, 2003). This process involves reading, writing, drafting, getting feedback, making changes, redrafting and so on in a cycle. In these early stages the process is a more cosy and friendly one than it should be at later stages when writing will need feedback from new audiences and (as one of my students put it) students start to 'expose themselves'. But the general aim of inducting students into the writing process – and learning, or re-learning, the rules, conventions and traditions of scholarly writing – is an important goal in these early stages.

Becoming part of a research community – avoiding isolation

One of the first aims, with help from the supervisor, should be to make the effort to become part of the research environment and research culture of (first) the department and (second) the university as a whole. In practical terms this can mean attending research seminars, meeting people in common rooms or student rooms, looking out for events run by the Graduate School or similar set-up, and simply finding critical friends who are prepared to read your work or just listen to you.

If there is not a programme of student-led seminars (and there should be in an active department) then students can be proactive and set one up themselves. It is often best to have a programme which centres on students presenting only to their peers, although the presence of a staff chair or the supervisor can be a help. These can be valuable for students for three reasons:

1 Gaining practice in presenting your work and exposing it to new eyes and ears.
2 Practising oral skills – these will be needed in the eventual viva voce (see later chapter).
3 Receiving feedback and encouragement from what should be a friendly and supportive audience.

Presentations at seminars such as these can be excellent preparation not only for the oral examination or the upgrade viva but also for the time when a student wishes to present to a wider audience of new faces at a conference.

Networking in the department and across the university is an excellent first step in feeling part of a research community – but the next phase is to network more widely: first, in the national community in your field; and secondly, probably involving e-mail or other electronic communication, the international networks in the area of study. Attendance at conferences, either at home or overseas, is an essential part of the networking process, although money is an object here (many departments can offer financial support for attending and presenting at conferences).

Of course, there are important practical differences for part-time students as compared with full-time, and campus-based students compared with remote location or 'distance' students. For some part-time students, perhaps on a professional doctorate, there are opportunities to meet at (say) weekend programmes or study schools. But for others there may be a pressing need to use the ICTs (information and communication technologies) available, whether it be something as basic as e-mail, a social network or Skype, for example. Again, students can be proactive and innovative here in setting up their own discussion groups, chat facilities and conferences using to a large extent whatever technology they choose (i.e. without having to be constrained by the choice of, say, virtual learning environment made by the institution).

In short, one of the aims of postgraduate work is sharing even if, and especially when, actual collaboration with others is not possible. Isolation, which in the past some doctoral students have complained about, should never be allowed to happen – this is the responsibility of both student and supervisor. The aim from the outset should be to become part of a community of practice (see later).

The importance of the 'affective domain'

The idea of an 'affective domain' is usually attributed to the American psychologist Benjamin Bloom who, with several colleagues, undertook an analysis of educational aims and objectives, classifying them into three broad areas: the cognitive, the affective and the psychomotor (Wellington, 2006: 24–9). Their resulting taxonomy has been widely used – arguably, its most valuable practical outcome has been to remind everyone involved in education (learners and teachers) of the importance of the affective domain in learning and personal development, i.e. of emotion, attitude, inspiration and motivation. We all appreciate that studying and writing at any level involves the cognitive domain (in short, skills, knowledge and understanding) but the importance of 'affect' can be neglected. In terms of action, the affective domain involves considering people's hopes and fears, giving people praise and encouragement and generally acknowledging that any educational development is an emotional process. The doctoral journey, with its ups and downs, the sheer hard work of writing, the occasional pain of receiving (and giving) feedback and the eventual oral examination is a classic example. And that is just the student: the affective domain for the supervisor in the whole process should also be remembered!

With this in mind, it is worth considering some of the anticipations of students as they embark on their postgraduate work. I have divided some of the sentiments expressed by students into two categories: hopes and fears.

Fears

Getting started

- Will what I am researching be substantial enough for doctoral level work?
- Staying sane; stuff that might happen on the way; abject failure
- Drowning in data
- Getting lost
- Going down too many wrong tracks/cul-de-sacs
- I will become boring – people's eyes will glaze over when I talk about my doctorate
- Losing touch with my supervisor
- Not getting on with my supervisor
- Lack of supervisor support
- The literature review: not doing it critically enough; drawing boundaries around it; getting confused or muddled by it

Worries over empirical work

- Gaining access to my participants or documents
- Not being able to find or gain access to enough research participants
- To develop skill in methodology and methods
- Not having a rounded understanding of different research paradigms

The viva

- Expressing myself properly in the viva
- Failing at the viva and needing another one

Writing worries

- My writing style and referencing/not being able to write well enough
- Not being able to find the right way of expressing/presenting/showing my work
- Writing the thesis
- Am I up to it? Getting it down on paper, using academic language
- Being seen by my supervisor as not good enough
- Lacking the courage to take risks
- Fear: that something really important is not picked up/noticed along the way
- Time management
- Leaving things to the last minute
- Things always take longer than we expect them to
- Keeping going and finishing!

Hopes

- To finish ... on time
- Staying focused, staying on track
- Good support from my supervisor and a good working relationship
- To stay motivated
- That my thesis makes a difference, even a small one
- To make a difference, to make a contribution
- To gain insight into my profession which will give value to my career, work and life
- That others will be able to relate to/identify with what I have written
- To learn, to enjoy it

Agreeing on the general ground rules

One of the issues to sort out at an early stage is how you and your supervisor will work together. Students should ask:

- What do you *want* from a supervisor?
- What do you *expect* from a supervisor?

But equally, students should reflect on and discuss with their supervisor:

- What will she/he *want* from her student?
- What will she/he *expect* from her student?

In my own discussions with students embarking on the doctoral journey I have come across a wide range of perceived needs, expectations and wants. Here are a few examples for you to consider:

- I want a hard worker, 'toughness', good guidance
- Consistency
- Signposting
- Guidance
- A critical friend
- I want the 'voice of experience'
- Awareness (from both sides)
- Directive (from some) … yet non-judgemental
- Helps to set deadlines (not just my responsibility)
- Open to my perspective … yet agenda setting
- Leaves space for my initiative
- Instills confidence, is confident him or herself
- A motivator
- Clear communication, clear feedback
- A balance between various things (as above and below)
- Dialogue
- Treats me as human
- To trigger creativity
- Realism
- A good listener
- Constructive critic
- Mutual respect
- Accessible
- I don't want any surprises at the end!

In basic terms, I have found that students' expectations of supervision can be classified under five main categories:

1 *Technical and organisational* – e.g. setting deadlines; 'where are you at?' reminders; a quick response; not changing the goalposts; target setting; help with university regulations; agreeing parameters; imposing deadlines.

2   *Practical* – e.g. on aspects of writing; practical ideas on methods, access, etc.; regular contact; a balance between informal and formal contact.

3   *Pastoral/affective* – e.g. praise; encouragement; empathy; support; tolerance: someone who will tolerate my ramblings; a safety net (am I doing OK?); interpersonal interaction; keeping me motivated; supportive criticism; showing an interest; reassurance; increasing collegial nature of meetings; inducting the student into professional academic practice.

4   *Methodological* – e.g. providing 'a road map'.

5   *Philosophical, theoretical, conceptual* – e.g. advice on focus; keeping me focused/keeping me on track; professional critique; a critical friend; boundaries; spotting the gaps; openness to new ideas; debate; clarifying things; pointers to the literature; highlighting different viewpoints; saving students from getting too caught up in their studies to see and recognise different points of view.

From the student's viewpoint

We finish this section on students' needs and expectations with two interesting comments for you to ponder from students at the start of their doctorate:

> My supervisor actually asked me at the start: 'how do you want me to supervise you?' And I thought that was brilliant. We did kind of negotiate how to work together and then worked at it … it kind of feels like an *old slipper* now, it feels quite comfortable. I tend to set the agenda for the meetings, it's mainly me. Again, that's because I trust her and I know she's bothered about me.

> You need to clarify expectations at the beginning – what are the student's expectations? what are the supervisor's? are they congruent? – if not then where are the disparities and how do you address those? It is useful to develop a time frame and to write a timetable … and agreeing frequency of meetings, contact outside of meetings – can I phone up, pop in, e-mail …?

From the supervisor's viewpoint

An equally important part of the supervision process, requiring equal consideration and discussion at the start of the journey, is the supervisor's perspective: What do they want? What do they expect? What do they get from supervising? Again, from my own experience of discussing this with supervisors, a range of responses is forthcoming. Supervisors say that they do it for enjoyment and to learn, to pick up some new references, new ideas, new methodologies … and so on. Many comment on the satisfaction that they gain from seeing a student 'through' from the first meeting to the eventual viva and perhaps to further publication.

One of my interviewees told me:

> Supervision gave me a major career development opportunity – it provided me with a real focus for the later stages of my career. I get a lot of satisfaction from it; I never feel that they have done it because of me, but I always take pleasure from their achievement. And I enjoy it, and I enjoy the learning.

Different supervisors have different views on how the supervision process should begin, and at later stages how it should develop, for example;

> I start from the point that whatever the student is going to do is going to be their work. I start from their interests, not mine.

> At first, the student really needs to feel confident with the supervisor. I think it's necessary to show them that you have a sufficient command of knowledge, and the experience to be able to supervise them. As the relation-ship goes on, I think one becomes more of a critical friend – the job is really then to offer critical advice and guidance, rather than feel that they are always looking for you for direction. At the end of course, it's mostly a case of critical readership.

Finally, supervisor and student should not forget that they can draw upon their colleagues in the department for such things as a second opinion, advice on aspects of the literature, suitable examiners and so on. The student they are supervising is not 'their' student alone.

Conducting, organising and planning meetings

A skills/training needs analysis and the skills agenda

An important part of the early meetings in the supervision process involves a kind of diagnostic discussion of the needs of the student in terms of (say) research methods, skills development and so on. For some universities this is formalised into a kind of 'skills and training needs analysis', with perhaps a form that has to be filled in and kept by both parties. In other cases, it may be less formal, requiring simply a discussion of what the student would like to do, which workshops to attend and so on. In many cases, for full-time PhD students, it may involve a commitment to an accredited programme of 'research training'.

A careful discussion needs to be held between student and supervisor on the issue of skills development. The push to develop 'generic, transferable skills' in postgraduate students has raised considerable heat. Some of the generic skills discussed have been presentation, communication, information literacy or ICT skills, collaboration and teamwork, and time management. Critics of this agenda have argued against it on several grounds, for example: first, that these skills cannot be divorced from the doctoral journey itself, i.e. they should be embedded in it; on educational grounds – they cannot be hived off and seen as generic, transferable and fit for all purposes, whatever the context, i.e. they are situated – some would go further and say that generic skills of this ilk are theoretically impossible. Thus it follows that they should not be seen as an 'add-on', something bolted onto the postgraduate programme. If they are, critics argue and many students concur, they may be seen as yet one more thing that has to be done. In other words, they will be a distraction from the main business of writing a dissertation, therefore a problem for time and energy and in turn a threat to timely completion. Supporters of the skills agenda have made several points: first, although some of these skills are embedded in the postgraduate journey, they are often seen as tacit, not-talked-about and unarticulated. It helps, they say, to make them clear and explicit, and for many students, additional courses and workshops can help to develop these skills which in turn will enhance their postgraduate programme.

The debate is set to continue and needs careful consideration in early meetings. However, there may be certain requirements imposed by the university which have to be met, whatever the student's and supervisor's views of the notion of generic skills.

Conduct

One of the key aspects of supervision to be clear about from the outset is the business of meetings and how they should be conducted. In particular, you should be involved in setting many of the ground rules for meetings, for example:

- Will you work from set agendas – and who will set them?
- How frequently should meetings happen?
- How will meetings be recorded?
- Will students (or supervisors) keep a progress log/a blog/a video diary/a reading log of the journey?
- How will targets and deadlines be set and decided on?
- Written work: what will be expected from both sides, e.g. how often, how detailed will corrections and feedback be?
- Who will gather and keep updating valuable information on 'outside' activities which can help both supervisor and student, for example: student networks, research networks, contacts, conferences, organisations and seminars?

Some authors have suggested the idea of setting up a *learning contract* at an early stage (Wisker, 2001: 55–60). This is a form of written agreement between both parties detailing (say) timelines, deadlines, duration and frequency of meetings, level of support, skill needs, shared and individual responsibilities, explicit expectations and so on. Wisker provides a full discussion with useful examples and templates for possible contracts of this kind. Both parties agree to it and sign it. The use of a contract may well be worth carefully considering in some situations.

Content

The content of meetings may be grouped into three main areas:

1 *Procedural issues* – e.g. frequency and duration of meetings, agendas, work setting, deadlines and so on.
2 *Academic issues* – these are at the heart of the process and are likely to include (at least) discussion of: the literature and how to handle it, what to read and what not to; theory and theoretical frameworks; debates on research design and methodologies; decisions on actual methods, sampling, gaining access and so on; structuring the dissertation work.
3 *Pastoral, social and personal issues* – e.g. managing time, keeping enthusiastic, juggling commitments.

The content of meetings in each of these areas will vary according to the phase of research the student is in. At all stages, a delicate balance in the supervisory process needs to be held in all three areas – this is discussed in the next chapter.

An unequal and complex relationship?

Some of the content for meetings suggested above will simply involve basic 'secretarial work', e.g. setting dates for the next meeting, keeping written records (either online or on paper). However, several aspects will necessitate careful and sensitive discussion, even something as basic as how often to meet and for how long. It needs to be remembered that the different perspectives in the supervisory relationship need to be recognised and reflected upon. In a sense, it is an unequal relationship: for the student, the thesis is the entire focus of their working life; for the supervisor, the student's work is one focus among many. It is also a complex one – probably more complex than the teacher–learner relationship and certainly as unpredictable. All supervisors and all students are different. Both sets bring variables with them ('baggage' to use the vernacular) such as gender, maturity, race, class, part-time or full-time status, personality, methodological and theoretical bias, past personal and professional experiences – and the unpredictable nature of the relationship as these two sets of variables combine will add to this variability. On a positive note, that combination should make the supervisory meeting more exciting, interesting, creative and productive! Incidentally, this variability means that the introduction (some would say imposition) of guidelines, formulae, precepts and regulations for the supervisory process needs to be handled with care.

Finally, it also needs to be remembered that any ground rules discussed at the early stages of the doctoral journey should not remain static. They should be considered and discussed in all the phases of the study (see next chapter).

Co-supervision – pitfalls and strengths

Many students embarking on a postgraduate degree may find that they have more than one supervisor. (I have even come across one case where a student told me that she had three.) If this is the case, then the importance of agreeing ground rules and deciding jointly about how to proceed is magnified. For example, with two supervisors, will you always meet together as a threesome? Will this always be possible? Will both supervisors do more or less the same job, e.g. will they both read each and every draft of your chapters? Will they both advise on (say): methodology, the literature review, data analysis ...? Or will one advise in one area of your work and one in another?

There are many other more general points to consider, for example:

- What is the value of co-supervision ... and what are its drawbacks? As a student, how should you handle co-supervision (see Table 3.1)?
- If you embark with one supervisor, is there perhaps a time when it may be valuable to bring in another? What timing will work best?
- How can a second supervisor make the process better? What dos and don'ts are involved? How does it change the process? Are there any drawbacks/pitfalls in joint supervision (see Table 3.1 for examples)?

Table 3.1 Positives and negatives in joint supervision

Positives	Negatives
Another reader	Contradicting each other – they don't always agree
Another viewpoint	Discussing your work between themselves
Good way to initiate a new supervisor	Logistics of arranging meetings for three
Maximise the strengths of each other	Not getting on
Work sharing, e.g. reading and commenting on written work in detail	Higher workload within a department if all students must be co-supervised
Covering for each other if necessary	Can there be a relationship if there are three or more (loss of intimacy)?

Becoming part of a community of practice

We have already mentioned that supervision should not be seen as a closed circle involving just student and supervisor(s). Part of the doctoral journey involves making full 'use' (in the nicest sense) of networks, peers, funding support, research cultures, critical friends, literature bases, library staff and other staff within or without the university. It is the joint responsibility of both student and supervisor to set up these links, especially to scholarly networks, at the outset of the programme and to maintain them for its duration.

Thus the general aim during a postgraduate programme is to become part of a community of practice. So, what is this and how can it be achieved?

A community of practice is an idea usually attributed to the work of Jean Lave and Etienne Wenger (1991) and to a later book by Wenger (1998). In a sense, it is a new term referring to a centuries old phenomenon. It refers to the notion of a group operating together with common purposes and shared practices as they learn and work together towards those aims or goals. These shared practices have emerged and evolved over time as the community has developed its own, often deeply embedded, ways of working or practices. As new people strive to enter the community they are to some extent on its margins and their activity at this stage has been described as 'legitimate peripheral participation'. Gradually, they may become inducted into the community to a greater extent as they experience its practices and become initiated into its 'rules', its ways of working, its language/discourse and so on. The idea of a community of practice has been commonly used in the context of discussing apprenticeship situations, e.g. for midwives, teachers, sailors, tailors and butchers. Learning in communities such as these is both social and situated, i.e. very much within a particular context (this relates to the notion of 'situated cognition' – see Wellington, 2006: 168–72).

It does have its uses in considering the doctoral journey although many would question whether the idea of a 'master and apprentice' should be associated with it. Its value in this context lies in reminding supervisors and students that learning:

- should be social and interactive rather than isolated and individual;
- is situated in a particular context or field;
- should involve communication and perhaps collaboration but certainly sharing;
- requires those involved to learn the rules of engagement (what might be cynically called the rules of the game – some of these rules, as we see in Chapter 5, are written and explicit but some are tacit and implicit); and
- leads to a fairly clear goal or endpoint (as with many other communities of practice such as midwifery or construction).

39

We should also remind ourselves than some communities of practice may have a sinister side and may even have an immoral purpose, e.g. white supremacy. Some may be exclusive, restrictive or gender-biased. Others may involve aggression or even bullying; some have initiation rites and unethical practices. One would hope that none of these sinister aspects could now apply to the doctoral journey in any context, from outset to viva to publication.

In practice, in the case of a postgraduate programme, becoming part of a community of practice is likely to involve:

1   Reading extensively, including reading past dissertations, attending conferences and seminars.
2   Using ICTs (information and communication technologies) in enhancing the doctoral process, e.g. learning environments, blogs, social networks, Internet sources and search engines, e-discussion groups, other modes of communication such as Skype and so on.
3   Drawing upon a range of other support systems in addition to your supervisor, such as:
    -   your peers on the doctorate – your peer network;
    -   other staff in the department or outside it;
    -   a 'critical friend' whom you can talk to and who will read your written work helpfully but critically – whatever stage you are at, if you don't have one, find one;
    -   family, friends, partners, spouses, cats, dogs, other animals?

In conclusion ...

This chapter has discussed the hopes, fears, needs and expectations of students as they embark on their postgraduate work. These need to be discussed and negotiated and the details of how they will be put into practice will differ from one supervisory relationship to another. However, my view is that the following expectations are all reasonable for a student to hold and to maintain throughout. Students should expect:

-   communication and exchange of ideas – a dialogue;
-   help with planning, goal setting and time management (long- and short-term);
-   their written work to be read in advance of meetings (provided they have given the supervisor reasonable time to read it);
-   constructive, honest feedback on and criticism of their writing;
-   responses to their queries, e.g. by e-mail, in a reasonable time;
-   guidance on fieldwork and issues of ethics and access;
-   advice on methodology and methods;

- help with networking, making contacts, becoming part of a community of practice;
- information on rules, regulations and forthcoming conferences;
- guidance on and preparation for the assessment process, written and oral.

As well as these practical and cognitive aspects of the supervision process, students should also expect interest, encouragement, praise, enthusiasm and confidence building – all part of the affective domain.

This chapter has looked at the important stage of the supervision process: getting started on the 'journey' and setting the ground rules. A study by Hockey (1997) showed that the supervision process involves a 'complex craft'. Supervisors and students are engaged in guiding, informing, critiquing, timing and foreseeing. Supervisor and student also engage in a kind of balancing act. We discuss this in Chapter 4.

 Further reading

Becker, L. (2004) 'Working with your supervisor', in *How to Manage Your Postgraduate Course*. London: Palgrave, Chapter 5.

Cryer, P. (2000) *The Research Student's Guide to Success*. Buckingham: Open University Press.

Wellington, J., Bathmaker, A., Hunt, C., McCulloch, G. and Sikes, P. (2005) *Succeeding with Your Doctorate*. London: Sage.

Wisker, G. (2001) *The Post Graduate Research Handbook*. London: Palgrave Macmillan.

4

Dealing with the complexity of the supervision process: striking the right balance

 Chapter aims

As mentioned in the last chapter, the experience of being supervised will be a very new one for most research degree students – this will be the first time you will work closely with the same academic or academics for a prolonged period of time. It is vitally important that you make the most of the supervision process and this in turn involves reflecting on it and discussing it.

This chapter looks in detail at:

- the process of supervision and the issues it raises;
- the delicate checks and balances needed for successful supervision – and the idea that this involves 'meta-supervision';
- phases of supervision as the work progresses;
- different styles of supervision that students may encounter;
- the vitally important interactions that occur in the supervision process, whether face to face or online.

Balance and mutuality

The title for this chapter comes from an excellent article by Delamont et al. in 1998. This was published over ten years ago but the issues it raised still apply in the current context. They talked about the delicate balances between 'interventionist' supervision and the student's autonomy, the imposition of control and the granting of licence, and the 'establishment of tight frameworks' and the student's need for 'freedom of manoeuvre'.

Finding a balance

Many aspects of supervision involve finding the right balance between certain characteristics and ways of behaving. For example, in my discussions with students many of them say that they want honesty from their supervisor – but when we explore this it does not mean that they either want or need their supervisor to say exactly what they think. Honesty can be brutal or it can be kind – brutal honesty is probably not a useful quality. To be frank is one thing, to be brutally frank is another. There are many other aspects of the supervisor–student relationship where a careful balance is required for a successful partnership; these can be grouped into three areas: *procedural*, *academic* and *pastoral*.

How do supervisors and students maintain a delicate balance between the extremes shown on the continua below; the first group is concerned with *procedural and academic matters*. With the first three we include the perspectives of students on this 'balance':

Leaving you alone to 'get on with it' …….. Pestering, reminding, cajoling you

I would hate to have somebody say 'you've got to produce something written every three weeks, you've got to do X amount of reading, go to this or that conference'… I'd have just given up. Then again, … 'laissez-faire' would be no good for me. You do get a little bit lost and you do need regular meetings to get some clarity again.

Someone pestering me all the time would make me feel anxious about my work … but if I had a laissez-faire person I'd also feel anxious, thinking 'Oh my god, have I done enough?'

Setting strict deadlines ……………. Allowing you to manage your own time

Being given deadlines just wouldn't work with me – because I have to go where my thinking leads me. I am at a certain age and I trust myself and I know how I work. So if I'm not ready to write I simply can't do it … when I'm ready to write that's where my real thinking takes place. But I have to do this almost like 'groundwork' and preparation first. If someone were to force me to write, yeah, I could do it … but I don't think I'd be producing good work. I want guidance rather than deadlines, as in 'you might find it useful to do this'. I suppose I am self-disciplined.

I need structure to work, I need to set myself goals; I put in my diary when I'm going to be working and on what. I need regular deadlines but with some flexibility – and not deadlines on a week-by-week basis, that would be too stringent. Being a parent makes me more conscious of time, I have to really plan when I can work and when I can't.

Directing, dominating your work.................Facilitating ... or leaving you to it

I think that as a student you know what you're looking at and you need to develop your ideas, so to that extent you need to be left to explore them ... but also the supervisor can make really good recommendations and can lead you into areas that you wouldn't have thought of; you can explore different avenues and widen your knowledge. But if the supervisor is saying every week 'read this chapter or read that chapter' then it wouldn't be your PhD, it would be the supervisor's.

Similar ways of expressing these extremes will be:

Keeping a healthy momentum going................... Rushing or over-hurrying things, e.g. fieldwork or writing

Prescription, direct guidance, power .... Student autonomy

Between being a manager, a director or even a dictator.....Or being too laissez-faire and the opposite?

Following the supervisor's interests .... Or the student's interests

Teaching.....Simply letting the student 'get on with it'/benign neglect
(Delamont et al., 1998: 160)

As far as the *pastoral* aspects of the supervision process are concerned, how is a balance to be maintained between the following?

Over-interested, patronising and intrusive .... Indifferent, disinterested, uninterested

Being sociable .... Aloof

Being caring ...... Disdainful (Johnson et al., 2000)

Keeping personal distance .... Closeness/intimacy

Being over-friendly, intrusive .... Dispassionate

The comments below express views from the student's perspective:

It could be more hurtful if your supervisor is your friend and you disagree – but they're not your friend, they're your supervisor; they are there to be honest about your work and get you through your PhD.

I think it depends on the kind of person you are; where people set the bounds of their privacy is different. I think this is where you've got to be compatible with your supervisor. If you don't have that compatibility it could cause problems ... And the relationship doesn't exist in a vacuum – you need to think about how it might look to the outside world.

I do appreciate that supervisors have limited time – but it's how it's handled that matters. If you're made to feel 'my time is precious and you're only a PhD student, so I will allocate you 45 minutes' ... if it comes across like that it would be very demoralising.

It's a relationship; you can't set it in stone because circumstances change. I've changed; my way of thinking has changed. I've learnt, that's the whole point. It would be sad if you did stay the same, wouldn't it?

I think it should be a professional thing – if the student just felt that they were 'part of the job' then it wouldn't be very encouraging or motivating. You need someone who will discuss your ideas with you and be interested in them, and critique them and support them ... and make you feel that you're doing something interesting and worthwhile. I think emotions come into it a lot – when you get feedback on your work, that's a very emotive process.

The writing process

There are also delicate balances to be considered when it comes to the important business of writing the dissertation (which we look at in detail in Chapter 7). It can be expressed crudely as:

> Allowing your writing to be 'yours'......... Your supervisor correcting, editing, rewriting, even adding

The key question is: what do you want or expect from your supervisor when it comes to feedback on written drafts? The supervisor's view needs to be discussed here and agreed upon as it could vary between completely rewriting a student's draft, correcting and suggesting, through to the more laissez-faire approach of simply expecting the student to 'self-correct'.

If the first extreme is taken, then the question is posed: whose dissertation will it be? Whose writing is it? If the latter extreme is taken in the supervision process, then how will your writing develop and improve? Will you, as a famous golfer once said, simply end up practising your faults?

We finish this section with two student perspectives:

> I like someone to do close proof reading. I trust my supervisor, sometimes she will say 'I don't understand that sentence' and I have to rethink it. I have to say she's always right! This is why trust is so important ... but it's got to be 'your voice' in your writing. I wouldn't want anything that leeched my voice out of it.

45

I wouldn't want someone going through every sentence and correcting every word because then it's not your voice any more; the words, they're your choice. However, if a sentence doesn't make sense because I have used words incorrectly or because my grammar is inaccurate, I would definitely want to know.

'Mutuality'

There are other characteristics of supervision where the key idea is that of mutuality, as well as balance ... for example, patience. It is important for a supervisor to be patient (but probably not too patient) but this quality should be mutual, i.e. it may apply equally to students. Thus you may need to be patient with a supervisor, especially at certain times of the year, e.g. in waiting for a supervisor to read and give feedback on written work. Equally, students should not be too patient with their supervisors, e.g. if they wait several weeks to get feedback on a draft chapter. You may also need to be patient with yourself, e.g. in not rushing things in a desperate need to 'get finished'. Thus the quality of patience requires both balance and mutuality.

Similarly, other qualities need both balance and mutuality, for example:

- praise – students will benefit from praise where praise is due; equally, supervisors thrive on praise, where it is merited;
- honesty, openness;
- respect;
- guidance;
- pressure;
- enthusiasm;
- involvement and interest.

Balances from the student's perspective: power, authority and advice

If we view the supervision process solely from the student's angle, there are a number of delicate balances which the student needs to reflect on. I show these below as two possible extremes on a continuum in the three areas to consider: the questions of power, authority and advice:

1 Power

Complete deference from student, subservience.................. Student 'precocious', over-confident, has false sense of independence

2   Authority

Supervisor in 'total authority' as well as an authority .... Student also
an authority as well as sometimes in authority

3   Advice and guidance

Student heeds advice slavishly, deferently .... Ignoring advice,
blind independence

With all of these three issues, the position adopted will depend on the
phase and stage of the journey and on the individuals involved – and
the relationship between them. In most cases, the ideal position will be
somewhere between the two poles. For example, with advice the best path for
the student is likely to be to take advice carefully and reflectively and to use
it judiciously rather than slavishly. With power, a position of complete
deference is unlikely to be productive, while equally a false sense of
independence and a feeling of not needing guidance and feedback will be just
as unhelpful. You and your supervisor need to recognise your own identity
and efficacy (rather than 'power' perhaps) in the supervision process.

   Finally, the issue of authority tends to be resolved somewhere along the
way in a successful supervision process – as many supervisors testify, the
student is likely to be an authority on his or her chosen area of study as a
result of the doctoral journey and many will say that their knowledge and
expertise in that area will exceed the supervisor's by the time of submission.

Reconciling the supervisor's goals and your aspirations

Sometimes there may be a delicate balance between the supervisor's own
goals, intentions, aspirations and research agenda and your own. Supervisors
may say that they want the student 'to write their own PhD, not mine' – but
on the other hand, most supervisors have research pressures themselves,
some intrinsic and some external or extrinsic. They have their own interests
and their own venture which they wish to pursue and it can be very tempting
(and very valuable) to bring the student into this venture.

   How can this show itself? It becomes evident in several areas: in choosing
the topic or pointing towards a topic and focusing it down; in the literature
review – if a supervisor is asking or directing the student to search for reading in a certain area; in the data collection, e.g. advising on one methodology
rather than another; in guidance on specific methods or research tools which
perhaps resonate with the supervisor's; in data analysis, e.g. in exploring,

trying or evaluating a tool or a program which the supervisor may wish to know more about.

Meta-supervision

In summary, all of the above balances need to be maintained, recognised and discussed during supervision. This kind of discussion about the supervisory process itself can be called (to coin a term) 'meta-supervision' or reflexive supervision. The balances are discussed and the relationship reflected upon by asking along the way: How is it going? Could the supervision be improved? And so on.

Equally, some of the tacit, unspoken aspects of supervision, e.g. the power and authority relationship, could be brought out into the open and made less tacit. These unspoken goings-on during supervision have been referred to as a kind of 'invisible pedagogy' – the aspects of guidance, direction, steering and feedback which go on and have major influence but somehow remain unarticulated. Meta-supervision, i.e. reflecting on and discussing the supervision process itself from time to time, can help to bring out the invisible processes that are taking place but which are so important to the doctoral journey. Meta-supervision may also help to pre-empt or prevent any conflicts and issues that might arise or cure any which have already arisen. (We discuss these possible issues in Chapter 6 under the heading 'What could possibly go wrong?')

What is all this talk about autonomy and/or dependency?

A lot is said and written about the move from dependency to autonomy as students progress through their thesis stage ('being weaned away from dependency into autonomy'). Personally I am not happy with these baby-like metaphors of weaning, or decreasing dependency. It is true that people do develop enormously in many ways during supervision but my line is that there is no time at which students or staff should become totally 'autonomous'. You should certainly not be in a state of isolated autonomy at any point. You should maintain and use the support systems that have been in place since phase one. You should keep in touch with your supervisor at all stages (she or he is being paid a salary at the end of every month, partly to supervise). Students should not try to be completely independent at any stage, right through to the final draft of your thesis and up to the day of the viva. Of course, you should not be over-dependent on any one person – but on the other hand, why should anyone work autonomously when you can have critical friends, a supervisor and a network of peers? It is also clear that your autonomy will vary according to the phase or stage that your research work has reached.

Johnson et al. (2000: 145) are similarly critical of the old notions of autonomy and independence. These ideas (or ideals) simply do not fit into the current debate on new modes of knowledge and new concepts of knowledge production. Knowledge is increasingly being produced in collaboration with others, by addressing problems in their context and involving inter-disciplinary approaches. The idea of the lone scholar working away on her or his PhD (a 'disembedded and disembodied figure driven by the love of ideas and scholarship': Johnson et al., 2000: 146) is no longer tenable. Incidentally, this also throws into question old concepts of the student being 'original', a concept which we consider in later chapters.

Phases of supervision

One of the important points to consider in reflecting on and making the most of supervision is the fact that most research journeys can be pictured as taking place and evolving through different stages and phases. There is no hard and fast rule about, say, exactly which phase a student will be in at a certain time – but generally, the journey can be seen as involving the following stages:

- *Phase 1: Getting started*
  - Becoming clearer about your title and research topic; focusing down – sorting out its scope and its boundaries, drawing a line round your project, making it do-able.
  - Refining and focusing your research questions; developing a conceptual framework: what theories or theorists are you likely to use? getting into a working routine and sorting out your personal time management; getting clear about your methodology and methods; making plans for data collection, e.g. sample, gaining access, timing, ethical issues; doing some early writing and reading; forming a working relationship and a pattern with your supervisor, including a system for record-keeping.

- *Phase 2: The middle phase*
  - Data collection; early data analysis; critical reading and writing around the literature; building up your references; keeping regular contact with supervisor; keeping records of supervision, either online or face-to-face contacts; using other support systems; writing chunks/chapters and getting regular feedback on your writing from your supervisor; overcoming obstacles.

- *Phase 3: The home strait*
  - Finishing data analysis; keeping regular contact; continued reading; presenting at conferences when you're ready; developing oral skills for the viva; writing the concluding chapters, the discussion and the implications (the 'so what?' bit); completing a first draft for someone to comment on (supervisor plus one other?).
  - Completing the final thesis; final proofreading and polishing its presentation; discussing examiners; preparing for the viva.
  - The viva.

Each stage involves different activities, styles of thinking, types of writing and needs for advice and supervision. Each phase will involve different expectations from both sides; each stage will involve a different level of dependence or independence from the student. Each phase will involve a different mode of supervision and different interactions during supervisory meetings – these modes or styles, and the interactions involved, are considered in the next three sections. But first, what do supervisors and students think of the idea of phases and stages?

From the supervisor's perspective

Among my interviewees, views varied widely. One was supportive of the idea:

> On the whole there are predictable phases, so I would be more inclined to call them stages, because they can often be anticipated. At first there is the initial enthusiasm that students bring to the study – then about six to nine months in they become frustrated if they're not moving forward as fast as they thought they would – and that can lead to a certain amount of disorientation, demotivation and confusion. Then there's the phase when they are required to produce a piece of substantive writing, which they find very difficult indeed, for all sorts of different reasons, especially as they become more provisional rather than as certain as when they began the project. Once they have achieved that first piece of writing, for example if they are doing it to upgrade to a PhD that can be a great boost. It can change the character of the supervision thereafter. Then I think the next phase is when they begin to lose stamina, especially for part-time students, perhaps after two years. That can be a lengthy phase of demotivation that you need to be patient with. Then the final phase is the attempt to produce a final draft and this can lead to frustration too.

Another was slightly more sceptical:

> I think there are implicit stages. Often a full-timer can follow a more linear pattern – they can spend a lot more time exploring the literature before they

have to plunge into the fieldwork. I would see the phases in terms of the structure of the thesis – but all theses are very messy and it never goes to plan, so the messiness differs from student to student. If they are doing an empirical study it depends so much on whether they can get the access to the people and places they want to go ... and that takes huge amounts of time and they are never, ever prepared for that. Students can find that very stressful. And for me, that's where the biggest support from the supervisor comes in.

A third described the notion as 'too linear':

It's different with different students really. A model of 'phases' may not be helpful – there are movements in different directions all the time. The supervisor has to be very aware of what the student wants at different times. Sometimes students want a sense of you giving them directives ('just do this'); other times they really don't need this or want it. It's very difficult for a supervisor to know what to do at different times. A model of phases is too linear. For example, students sometimes come with a clear view of what they want to do; sometimes they don't. And even if they come with a clear view, so they start from a position of confidence, that can change very quickly when they realise that their focus was perhaps too general, and going into the literature more and more can start to bring up uncertainties about what it is they are doing. And sometimes students who come, apologising for the fact that they don't know exactly what they're looking for, sometimes they find their feet very quickly.

There is a kind of spiral. Even at the end you can still feel very uncertain about what you've done as a doctoral student – and especially facing the viva, all your doubts return ... and at that point again the supervisor role is very important.

From the student's perspective

Again, views vary. For some the idea may be helpful:

The first element is your literature review, and then that feeds into your methods, then you home in on your questions; that will lead you to your next stage which is 'what are the best ways to answer those questions'; so you will be developing your research tools and gaining access ... and then the next stage will be actually going in and doing your field research. Ethics will go right through from beginning to end; analysis will happen from day one as well, but there will be a discrete stage as well when you're doing a more specific, focused analysis. And the final part will be the final 'writing up' – maybe this should be called editing. So the ethics, analysis, writing and reading will be from day one really, right through. So there are stages that are imagined, but in reality some things carry on all the way through.

But it is helpful to think of those stages, to help you get through. Otherwise the whole process could seem unmanageable.

For others it may be too 'crude':

I personally think it's too crude – for me there has been a lot of 'to-ing and fro-ing'. I suppose there are phases in the sense of *being ready* to do certain things, such as writing a chapter. But it's more like being on a spiral, adding layers all the time; sometimes it feels like I've gone back to the same place but it's only that I'm in the same spot but higher up!

Moving to a new phase via the 'upgrade process'

Many university departments adopt the practice of asking their doctoral students to go through an upgrade procedure before they can go full steam ahead with their doctoral studies. This is often used if students first register in a department as an MPhil student – they are then asked to submit an upgrade paper before they can proceed to PhD. But it can also be used in a professional doctorate before a student can proceed from the 'part one stage' (often involving a number of written, assessed assignments based on taught modules) to the stage of conducting their own, in-depth research leading to a dissertation, i.e. in moving from part 1 to part 2 of a professional doctorate. In the case of part-time students this is normally after 24 months but can take place earlier for a PhD upgrade if the supervisor feels it is appropriate. In the case of full-time students, e.g. moving from MPhil status to PhD, then normally the upgrade procedure would take place after 12 months; again it can take place earlier if the student is ready. The process may sound rather daunting to a student, especially as it often involves writing an 'upgrade paper', followed by a face-to-face meeting of some sort, rather like a viva. In fact, the whole process should be of great benefit to everyone, as this section explains.

Why have an upgrade?

The upgrade process should be valuable to the student, the supervisor and the department. One of the aims of the upgrade is to act as a kind of assessment; the other two aims are much more formative – in providing feedback to the student and the supervisor(s) and offering practice:

1 *Assessment.* The upgrade should provide an opportunity to ensure that the work which you have done so far indicates that you are capable of carrying out research at doctoral level. Is the planned project worthy of taking to this level? Does it have the potential ('mileage', as some people express it)? Does the

student show the potential capability of succeeding at doctoral level, including the eventual *viva voce?*

2   *Feedback.* Staff involved in the upgrade should give formative feedback and guidance to the student on (for example) her/his writing, oral presentation, literature coverage, methodology, ethical issues, scope and focus, future plans and timetable. The upgrade process also provides valuable feedback to supervisors – it may well be the first time that the student and supervisor have gone public and opened out their work to a new audience for comment and helpful criticism.

3   *Practice.* Finally, the upgrade should also be seen as an opportunity for the student to develop and improve her/his oral skills and presentation, i.e. to practise for the viva.

What is an 'upgrade paper'?

Many departments will ask students to write an upgrade paper. The main purpose of the paper is to demonstrate your capability to carry out an in-depth study. (Incidentally, parts of any student's writing for the upgrade paper may well be used in the final thesis, often after adaptation.) Students are typically asked to produce an upgrade paper of around 10,000 words (plus or minus 10 per cent) which is likely to include:

- some discussion of the existing literature in the area and its importance in the proposed study: this is not meant to be the definitive text but students must demonstrate that they have a good grasp of key literature in the area, even if they are not yet fully engaged with all the arguments;
- a statement of the aims of the study: these should be as clearly articulated as possible. The paper should include some discussion of the methodology including theoretical and analytical frameworks which are to be used. Of course, at the upgrade stage, you may still be clarifying your focus;
- some discussion of the proposed methods of study and ethical issues which may arise;
- full references to research and secondary sources which have been used as well as those still to be accessed;
- a draft structure for the proposed dissertation itself, including chapter headings and a short summary of content for each chapter;
- a timetable for the study including an estimate of likely completion date;
- any questions that the student would like to pose to upgraders during the viva.

Procedures for the upgrade process

Often the supervisor will approach two preferred upgraders from within the department to see if they are willing and able to help. Ideally, one upgrader may be chosen on the basis of their knowledge of the subject area and the second upgrader might be chosen for their methodological expertise. This is so that the student can discuss any particular substantive or methodological issues which they are still struggling with or are unclear about. Upgraders should, once they have read the upgrade paper, meet together to discuss how they want to conduct the viva.

The supervisor should be present at the viva, although she or he will not participate in the discussion unless invited to by the upgraders. The supervisor should usefully take notes about important points made by the examiners, such as advice given. In many departments, students are allowed to audio-record the upgrade if they wish and in my experience this can be very valuable.

Decision-making

The entire upgrade process should be of great benefit to the student and the supervisor(s). A fresh pair of eyes, or two pairs, have looked at the proposed research questions, planned methods and literature base. In most cases, the student and supervisor can then proceed to the dissertation stage with the guidance and formative feedback given by the upgraders acting as a kind of 'springboard' or stimulus to move ahead.

In rarer cases where there are serious concerns over the standard or potential of the proposal, upgraders should give clear guidance after the upgrade viva as well as in a written report. If the upgraders are not convinced that the student is ready to proceed to the final dissertation stage it is important that they say so – it is a disservice to the student and the supervisor to gloss over any potential problems and allow them through to the final phase in an attempt to be kind (and, from my experience, this can create a lot of eventual stress for the student and staff supporting and supervising).

In cases where the upgrade paper itself is weak, in terms of substantive and/or methodological understanding, students may well be advised to amend and resubmit their paper. In extreme cases it may be necessary to hold another upgrade viva. In less extreme cases, requiring minor amendments or additions, it is the responsibility of the supervisor to work with the student in ensuring that the resubmitted paper answers the concerns raised in the upgrade report.

Styles of supervision

Several authors have presented a range of styles of supervision which different supervisors may adopt, or in some cases the same supervisor may adopt at different times and in different phases of the research journey. It is worth considering these alleged styles in analysing the supervision process; however, they should not be treated as anything more than a valuable way of reflecting on the interactions that occur, i.e. they are not helpful if used as a way of labelling or pigeon-holing a particular supervisor.

One classification is provided by Anne Lee (2008), based on her research into the supervision process. She suggests that there are five main approaches to supervision:

1 *Functional* – in this approach the main purpose is project management.
2 *Enculturation* – here, the emphasis is on encouraging and developing the student as a member of the research community (see the discussion elsewhere in this book on communities of practice).
3 *Critical thinking* – the emphasis is on developing the student's ability to question and evaluate their own work (and that of others, in my view), i.e. to develop the ability to be critical.
4 *Emancipation* – the student is encouraged by her supervisor to develop her own thinking and ideas – this relates to the discussion of autonomy and independence elsewhere in this book.
5 *Relationship development* – a rapport is developed between supervisor(s) and student involving enthusing, inspiration and caring (cf. the affective domain discussed in this book).

Lee's paper (2008: 271–7) goes on to provide helpful illustrative quotes from her interviews to show how these approaches are put into practice. She also reports the 'tensions' that supervisors try to reconcile between their professional role and their personal self in the supervision process, and between the need to support student (dependence) and the goal of developing independence and 'emancipation'. These reported tensions are similar to the delicate balances mentioned above.

Lee's 'concepts of supervision' are useful for both students and supervisors to consider in making the most of the supervision process. However, they should not be used as labels to designate a certain supervisor as 'functional', 'emancipatory' or whatever – although some supervisors do veer towards some of Lee's five approaches more than others. My own experience is that a good supervisor can and should adopt all of these approaches at different times and phases of the supervision process – and this should be encouraged and even asked for by the student. There will be times when a functional approach, e.g. devising a schedule, setting deadlines, agreeing a timetable, is required. At other times, enculturation will occur in, for example, deciding on conferences to attend or to present at, seminars to go to or journals to aim for in getting work published. The third approach, developing critical thinking, is essential in supervision in order for a student's work to reach doctoral level, since most criteria for 'doctorateness' require criticality (see Chapter 6); similarly with emancipation:

work at this level requires questioning existing work and thinking, putting forward new ideas and developing new ways of seeing things. Finally, supervision inevitably requires encouragement, praise, enthusing and inspiring – especially in periods of the doctoral journey where doubts begin to creep in and the end seems distant (see Chapter 5 of this book).

It will be a great help to students and supervisors to be aware of these approaches and the need for them at different times during the supervision process.

Taylor and Beasley (2005: 63–5, drawing on Gatfield, 2005) also provide a valuable discussion of what they call 'supervisory styles'. Their starting point is that every supervisor has their own, often implicitly held, assumptions about what supervision involves and this leads to their 'preferred supervisory style'. This starting point may be debatable, especially if it were to lead to labelling of a supervisor as one type or another, but it is certainly worth considering from the student's point of view: does your supervisor have a certain style? How does it relate to your own needs and aims?

What about the issue of whether there is a match or congruence between a supervisory style and the needs of a particular student (Malfoy and Webb, 2000)? Would the presence of such a match make it acceptable for a supervisor to adopt a certain style? For example, if a supervisor's style is *laissez-faire* ('let them get on with it') is this approach acceptable if the student is able to manage and direct him or herself and is also able to find their own support and resourcing? My own answer would be no, for at least three reasons. First, how do supervisors and students know their own needs? Second, the needs of every student will vary over time, according to the phase they are in. And thirdly, no matter what the self-management skills and independence of the student (a highly problematic notion anyway) it is not acceptable for a supervisor to adopt a totally laissez-faire approach.

The idea of styles is an interesting one and the discussion above should help you in reflecting on your own supervision and how to obtain the most value from it. However, the notion that any supervisor can adopt a certain style is no longer tenable (even if it ever was). The key requirements now are two fold: adaptability and flexibility (Pearson and Brew, 2002). Different approaches need to be followed at different phases; different styles, if this is the right word, need to be followed with different students. No two supervision processes will be the same.

From the supervisor's perspective: are there styles of supervision?

I see evidence of different styles when I take over from somebody else. Once I took over from someone and was very surprised at how 'technical' they were. I always offer students a drink when they first come in, especially part-timers who may have come some distance. This person I took over from was very much: this student arrives at 2.30 p.m., I give them 45 minutes, this is the form we filled in last time, we agreed that you would do X and Y, then go through a draft page by page. Then five minutes before the 45 were up it was a case of: what are the goals for next time, fill in the new form and off you go. This person would arrange their day so that they had, say, three tutorials one after another ... and they were all exactly the same. What I learnt from that was that I could tighten up things in some ways – but on the other hand I knew it was not my style. So clearly, there are different styles. And when I externally examine, there are obviously very different styles because you will hear people in vivas and you start to read between the lines and realise they've not seen much of their supervisor.

I would call it a preference myself. You can see differences; people in the past have tended to be far more directive and far more negatively critical than I would try to be. They were far more willing to tell people that what they had submitted in draft was wrong and they would have to do it again. I have seen transfer reports here where some colleagues set out to be negative – as if they are trying to demonstrate that they have a greater repository of field knowledge than the student. People like that are still in the system but I think that people newer to the system have tended to be less judgmental and more supportive – and I think that's due to changes in the whole sector of higher education.

Metaphors for the supervisor

My own preference in reflecting on the doctoral journey is to consider which metaphor might be most appropriate for the supervision process at any time (given that it does vary). Consider the following metaphors:

- a guide (e.g. over a mountain range, but not to carry your luggage for you, or through the 'doctoral maze'), a critic;
- a friend, an adviser, devil's advocate (putting the opposite side of things);
- a manager, a coach, a gatekeeper, a holiday rep;
- a sounding board, a mirror, a counsellor (like a marriage counsellor perhaps?);
- a mentor and his or her apprentice (learning the craft of research);
- a marriage between two partners, a parental relationship (maternal or paternal);
- the supervisor as a clock.

I have heard all these metaphors expressed by either students, e.g. the clock notion, or by staff. I leave it up to the reader to decide which of the above might best fit their supervision process in its different phases and stages.

One of my interviewees summed up her view of her role by saying:

I see myself as a critical friend – I am some people's mummy too, but not everybody's. I also feel I am a mentor and a facilitator.

Another said: 'My job is to have faith in my student and to convey that faith to them.'

Interactions in the supervision process

Face-to-face meetings

We have looked at phases and styles of supervision, followed by a consideration of some of the metaphors that might be used to picture and help us think about the supervision process. One final way of considering supervision, with the aim (as always) of maximising its benefits, is to examine what actually goes on during the business of supervision. In other words, we can reflect about the actual interactions that take place in supervisory meetings, online discussion or other kinds of communication. An article by Wisker et al. (2003), based on research into supervision meetings, examined what they called 'supervisory dialogue interactions' (p. 97). These were divided into nine categories: didactic, prescriptive, informative, confronting, tension relieving/social, eliciting, supporting, summarising and collegial exchange. These types of exchange relate neatly to the notion being used in this chapter that most communication can be divided into procedural, academic and pastoral/social.

From my own experience, I would add the following types of interaction which occur during supervision, many of which overlap with the categories above:

- questioning/asking
- diagnosing
- criticising
- commenting
- feeding forward
- getting started
- looking forward
- looking back/'recapping'
- thanking
- reporting
- counselling
- digressing
- challenging
- summarising
- countering
- feeding back
- socialising
- rounding off
- planning ahead
- apologising
- informing/telling
- advising
- consulting
- storytelling.

Clearly, the presence and actual nature of these interactions depends on the relationship between supervisor(s) and student – for example, the workings of power or deference between one and another. Some interactions are likely to be led by the supervisor, such as criticising, feeding forward and commenting – others may be initiated by the student, such as reporting and consulting.

Equally, the occurrence and frequency of these interactions will depend on the phase of the research journey. Thus diagnosing and eliciting are likely to occur at an early stage, for example when training/development needs are discussed and analysed. On the other hand, detailed criticising and challenging during supervision will be more common during the latter stages such as writing the thesis and preparing for the viva, while many of the social interactions (thanking, apologising, storytelling) will occur at all phases of the process.

Interaction during online supervision – and its issues

Chapter 2 discussed the impact of globalisation (with its two key facets of rapid travel and electronic communication) and this has been one of the major factors in increasing the diversity of students mentioned already. This has important implications for the supervision process that we have been considering in this chapter.

Another effect of globalisation is that many students may take an undergraduate degree in their own country but of necessity must go to the so-called developed countries to progress to a masters or a doctorate, at the high, expensive end of the market. This often results in having to travel back and forth to their own country in order to collect data for an empirical study. The provision of programmes which allow students to be home-based, with staff from (say) a UK university providing two or three study schools per year and electronic contact and tutoring in between has provided a welcome opportunity for many overseas students, with (usually) lower fees. Alternatively, many universities offer 'remote location' programmes in which (typically) a student can remain in his or her home country and may be required to visit the university perhaps once or twice a year, with regular electronic contact in between. Data from Powell and Green (2005) suggest that in the UK, 45 per cent of research students are from other parts of the world, with figures of 25 per cent in France, 20 per cent in Australia and 14 per cent in the USA. These changes have had a huge impact on the nature of research degree programmes and, of course, the supervision process. For example, supervision now commonly involves more electronic contact, fewer face-to-face meetings, greater potential for isolation in some situations and different needs regarding motivation and the affective domain.

Many of the issues and conceptions presented in this chapter are as relevant in considering online supervision as they are for face-to-face (f2f) contact. For example, the types of interaction involved, e.g. questioning, clarifying, commenting or even confronting, will be as common and as important online as they are f2f. The categories of interaction, i.e. procedural, academic and pastoral, all need to be considered in reflection upon online supervision.

For example, encouraging, cajoling and praising students will be as important, and perhaps more so, when the contact is largely electronic. It is important for students to make the most of online supervision, and to reflect upon it, in the same way as you would with f2f contact. For most part-time students (and even full-time in my experience) the supervision process will involve a combination of both – in that case, the value and relative merits of the two means of communicating need to be considered and maximised. Face-to-face meeting will be more valuable than e-mail contact for certain interactions – certainly the social and pastoral aspects of supervision; on the other hand, many procedural aspects of supervision might best be handled (and recorded) using electronic contact. Perhaps when it comes to the real nuances of academic discussion, questioning and debate, a face-to-face dialogue may be essential. Whatever your situation as a student, you should 'weigh up' the pros and cons of each mode of communication carefully, and work out with your supervisor the optimal way of proceeding. This may include 'face-to-face' contact using computer technology such as Skype, often a useful compromise when supervision is at a distance.

In conclusion ...

This chapter has attempted to delve into the complexity of the supervision process, its different phases and the styles or interactions involved. By trying to reflect on this process and to conceptualise it, both supervisor and student can maximise the benefit of their meetings, whether they be f2f or online. It is clear that many delicate checks and balances are needed to make the experience a successful and productive one.

 Further reading

Delamont, S., Atkinson, P. and Parry, O. (1998) 'Creating a delicate balance: the doctoral supervisor's dilemma', *Teaching in Higher Education*, 3 (2): 157–72.
Lee, A. (2008) 'How are doctoral students supervised? Concepts of doctoral research and supervision', *Studies in Higher Education*, 33 (3): 267–81.
Wisker, G., Robinson, G., Trafford, V., Creighton, E. and Warnes, M. (2003) 'Recognizing and overcoming dissonance in postgraduate student research', *Studies in Higher Education*, 28 (1): 91–105.

5

What could possibly go wrong?

'The best laid schemes o' mice an' men/Gang aft a-gley.'
(From 'To a Mouse' by Robert Burns)

 Chapter aims

This chapter discusses:

- some of the obstacles and aids likely to be encountered along the 'personal journey' of doing a doctorate;
- some of the things that may not go according to plan ('gang aft a-gley');
- some of the activities and processes that can facilitate progress on the journey and some of the barriers to it.

The chapter also considers issues that may relate to supervisors, their circumstances and their approach to supervision – and issues that are more student-centred. Finally, we look at a framework for making sense of these issues with a view to dealing with them, wherever possible.

Introduction: facilitators and barriers

Attaining a postgraduate degree, especially a doctorate, is a major achievement – it requires industry, commitment, enthusiasm, endurance, perseverance, academic ability, time management, the capability to write at length and the oral skill to defend what you have written. This is a daunting set of requirements – and it faces all students. But there are many aspects of the supervision process which can play a major part in facilitating that achievement. Conversely, the absence of these factors can hinder that achievement.

In the early stages, good induction into the department and institution, initial focusing of the research topic (making it do-able), becoming part of a community of peers/fellow students, setting initial milestones/deadlines and agreeing ground rules with your supervisor(s) will be all be helpful processes. As your research journey proceeds, many other factors can aid progress: integration into the research environment and life of the department; broadening interactions across the department and university for wider advice and consultancy; networking nationally and internationally; keeping a healthy work–life balance; praise and encouragement; support from family and friends; advice and feedback on your writing at frequent intervals; a growing sense of independence, autonomy and ownership of the project in the later phases; and, towards the end of the journey, some guidance and discussion on 'where next', especially with a PhD when it is seen as part of a career strategy. One vital aid to completion throughout the process is if both sides – supervisors and students – meet their deadlines.

The above factors and processes can be major facilitators in aiding progress on the research journey. But, to paraphrase William Shakespeare, the course of a doctoral journey never did run smooth. Many factors and circumstances, often not of your own making, can impede progress. Adequate funding, not only for subsistence but also for things like attendance at conferences, can be a great facilitator; but equally, poor financial support can be a barrier, especially if it restricts access to resources, the ability to carry out empirical work in different places or the freedom to attend and present at conferences. More seriously, lack of finance may mean a student has to move to part-time status or even temporarily postpone their course. This applies not only to PhDs but also to professional doctorates.

A healthy work–life balance, with time spent away from research, can be a major facilitator but if life gets in the way of work then the research journey suffers. This can occur for all sorts of reasons: family complications, whether involving parents, partners, existing children, new children or grandchildren, are often the most common. This is especially true for part-time students, for mature students who perhaps have elderly parents at one extreme and children or grandchildren at the other to consider, and for professional doctorate students who may also be holding down a job in a senior position. In my experience of supervising mature students, the balls that some manage to juggle in the air can be truly remarkable.

Other, more specific, problems which can occur include: if students feel isolated as opposed to a member of a peer network or community; over-anxiety whatever the reason; if you have more than one supervisor and there is lack of coordination or, worse still, disagreement among the team; writing delays, procrastination and writer's block (all discussed in Chapter 7); and finally, uncertainty about your future while in the later phases of the research.

Finally, a key factor accounting for anxiety and delay for those undertaking empirical work is its sheer messiness (as we discussed in earlier chapters). A research project does not follow a straightforward, linear path but a cyclical, iterative one. This is especially true when it involves human beings. Research involving people, for example interviewing or observing, can lead to complications and sensitivities around access (one can never obtain quite the sample one would really like), response rates, consent or permissions, practicalities and complex ethical issues, especially if the work involves humans under the age of 18. Another factor sometimes leading to consternation comes as the data are being collected and considered. In some cases, the data may not be quite as you wanted, hoped for or expected. That can be an advantage if the data are interesting and unexpected but it can also cause anxiety if feelings arise about the data being too predictable, boring or mundane, as one of my students once put it when he was writing up. The data, as statisticians sometimes say, do not always behave themselves. Incidentally, this is often a matter of perception or being too close to it and in this case good supervision, reflection and discussion can help. But in other cases it necessitates going back to collect more data, perhaps in a different way or with a different sample – hence the cyclical nature of real research (see Wellington and Szczerbinski, 2008).

This introductory section has outlined a whole range of facilitating factors and their converse, hindrances and barriers. These are summed up in Table 5.1, with the key factors in later phases listed lower down in the table.

It is interesting to note that most of the facilitators and barriers in this table can be classified as academic, procedural or pastoral/social, i.e. using the same categories that we have used in previous chapters. An interesting article by Ahern and Manathunga (2004) used three similar groupings in discussing factors which hinder progress: cognitive, affective and social. Their article suggests means of overcoming them and, to use their metaphor, ways of 'clutch-starting stalled students'. One of those authors (Manathunga, 2005) suggested four types of behaviour which signal that students are 'stalling', to pursue this metaphor, in their research journey:

- frequently changing their focus or plans;
- avoiding communication with their supervisor;
- isolating themselves from peers and the department;
- avoiding submitting written work for comment.

In my experience, these are all common tactics when a student is facing some of the barriers in Table 5.1, e.g. finding it hard to balance work with life outside, time management, over-anxiety or other 'doctoral doubts', lack of funding and inappropriate supervision.

Table 5.1 Factors commonly facilitating and hindering the research journey

Facilitators to progress	Barriers
Good induction, needs analysis and initial planning	Poor induction, lack of diagnosis of needs
Good access to materials and resources	Poor access to resources
Adequate funding	Lack of funding
Agreeing ground rules and setting realistic milestones	Little agreement on goals and milestones
Writing support and feedback	Writer's block; little feedback on or support for writing (practising one's faults)
Healthy work–life balance and time out; support from family, friends and peers; self-care	Life prevents work; no support from family, friends, peers; domestic, paid work or emotional problems
Both sides meet deadlines	Student does not meet deadlines; supervisor not responding after an agreeable time; over-anxiety
Member of peer network, critical mass of students and healthy departmental research environment	Isolation and loneliness; no networking in the department or university
Networking and communicating nationally and internationally, e.g. conferences; online contact and discussion	No networking nationally or internationally
Active, supportive, regular supervision without it being overbearing or dictatorial	Poor supervision/lack of coordination or consensus across a team
Becoming independent, growing autonomy; increasing sense of identity and ownership of the work	Student left to own devices – false autonomy; questioning of identity or ownership of the work
Guidance on when to submit and 'where next'	Not knowing when to submit; no advice on the future; uncertainty and anxiety over where next

From the supervisor's perspective

What do supervisors see, from their experience, as the common obstacles faced by postgraduate students? Here are three examples from my interviews:

> Simply being able to manage time and tasks, in a way that lets them engage with their doctorate. As time goes on, with societal changes and economic pressures, this seems to have increased – the pace of the real world gives them a severe challenge. Financial problems, fees – most part-time students have a range of financial pressures. Life changes, jobs change, families grow ... none of which they have anticipated, and then they get almost torpedoed.

One gave a brief list:

> Personal issues; not able to stop reading; perfectionism; not being prepared to submit even though it's ready; insecurities.

Finally:

> Getting access for collecting data; time, especially part-time students; personal lives can be very unpredictable; losing interest in their topic – wondering 'why did I ever want to do this?' ... and circumstances change, e.g. policies, and they get distracted and want to go down a different alleyway. It's then difficult for them and the supervisor to try and keep it on track.

From the student's perspective

One student, in the early stages of her work, looked ahead to some of the problems she might face:

> Gaining access and getting consent; being overwhelmed – you can impose blocks on yourself by making it bigger than it is. If I get to the stage when I'm not enjoying my writing that might be a possible block; I think it's important that you enjoy what you're doing. If the supervisors don't think some of my ideas are worth pursuing, it's difficult then, if I don't follow their advice, because other people (such as examiners) might agree with them and not me.

Another student looked back at the obstacles that she had encountered so far:

> My family life did affect my work. It's difficult to separate your postgraduate research from the rest of your life. It **becomes** your life. I think supervisors need to recognise that, otherwise students could become quite devious in keeping it from them. My family problems did affect my work and it's good to be able to be honest with your supervisor about it.

In the next sections of this chapter we look in more detail at some of the factors presented and listed above – and discuss some of the strategies for overcoming them. One of the first things which can really help is to become aware of the possible pitfalls, procrastinations and avoidance strategies which can occur – and to reflect upon them. The purpose of this introduction has been to start this process.

Issues with supervisors

The 'I'm so busy' supervisor

> It really bugged me how professors constantly talk about how busy they are to a point where I personally didn't want to ask anybody for anything, and that ultimately can hold you back. It can really limit your experiences because you feel guilty all the time ... (Comment from a Canadian student, reported in Acker, 1999: 80, where she discusses 'faculty busyness')

As head of research degrees in my own department I have sometimes had students come to see me (or e-mail me) to tell me how busy their supervisor is – their visit to me to convey that information is usually a result of one or more reasons: the meetings themselves are too hurried and perhaps interrupted by phone calls or people knocking on the door, i.e. they are not satisfactory; the second reason may be that the meetings are too infrequent for the student's liking; the third may be that more than one meeting has had to be postponed, rearranged or at worst cancelled; and finally, the fourth reason – and most common in my experience – is that the student has sent the supervisor a piece of writing and has not had feedback on it within the time frame expected by the student.

My first response is always to say that of course they are busy, that's the nature of the job – most academic staff in my experience work extremely hard, for long hours and do not have clearly demarcated times between working and leisure hours (this is made most clear by my inbox for e-mail, with messages arriving at most times of the day or night). So yes, the supervisor is busy – but the key point is that supervising students is part of the job. It is not voluntary work; it is something that academic staff are paid to do. Moreover, in most cases, you (the student) are paying for it, unless you have a fee waiver or a generous sponsor. In short, a good working relationship has to be mutually agreed (and written down if necessary) about what is acceptable from both sides. The lines need to be drawn around the question of what is acceptable and what is not.

First, it is not acceptable for a supervisor (however busy) to allow interruptions to meetings, except in an emergency (this exception applies to all the points below). For example, the phone ringing in someone's room should never take priority over the live discussion (yet I have seen this happen many times, even or perhaps especially with mobile phones).

Secondly, there is no justification for a meeting being cut short – the student and supervisor should decide on a time, a duration and an agenda – and adhere to it.

Thirdly, although meetings will sometimes have to be postponed and rescheduled (by either party) this should be the exception rather than the rule. If it becomes the norm, then a student does have the right to complain.

Fourth, meetings need to be scheduled at a frequency which both 'sides' agree upon and which suits the current phase of supervision. For example, in the early stages of research more frequent contact is needed when the focus is being sharpened, plans are being laid and ground rules are being set. At later stages, data collection for example, the meeting frequency may be less. In the final phases, for example in finishing the writing, meetings will be largely about feedback and formative assessment of written work and will be of a different kind and frequency. All through the phases of the doctoral journey, these issues need to be jointly negotiated and mutually agreed.

Finally, the issue of the time between a student submitting a piece of writing and receiving feedback is always a contentious one. With our own writing, we would (myself included) all like our feedback to meet some key criteria: first, that it should be, ideally, immediate, but if not then in good time; secondly, it needs to be clear and specific, i.e. it should make sense and the writer actually knows what to do with it; and third, it needs to be constructive, encouraging and formative as opposed to being over-critical, dampening or gloomy and summative. It is feedback on work in progress. This is what the writer wants – in reality, supervisors are busy and need to be given time to provide feedback which has the above qualities. A student cannot expect a supervisor to provide good, formative feedback on a draft chapter within less than a week (though I have known students who have expected this). However, to wait five weeks for comments on a draft chapter is not acceptable – how can students be expected to finish on time and improve their university's record for completion rates if they have to wait for five weeks for feedback on each chapter of their dissertation? Again, the ground rules need to be negotiated on by both parties and they will involve some give and take on both sides. This will vary and will depend on the time of the year (students and supervisors usually like to have the occasional holiday), the phase in the supervision process and the current commitments of the supervisor. At some times he or she will be able to turn a chapter round more quickly than at others.

The key, as always, is to negotiate and to agree.

The 'do as was done unto me' syndrome – the need for reflective practice

A supervisor's own experience as a research student can be one major influence (among many) on their own practices, attitudes and approaches as a supervisor. It can work in at least two ways (Lee, 2008: 276, discusses this in some depth and comments that supervisors may seek to 'emulate, add to or avoid their own experience').

Some published studies on the supervision process report supervisors as describing what a bad, negative experience they had themselves as a student and making a determined effort to be better supervisors themselves. For example, Delamont et al. (1998) reported a range of supervisors who were committed to making their own supervisory practices far more positive than the attitudes, approaches and practices they had experienced as students. One of their interviewees stated that as a student he had 'no supervision at all' and as a result now feels 'strongly about care and attention'. He reported that he had been scarred by his own experience. The Delamont et al. article tells of doctoral supervisors frequently recounting horror stories about their own doctorates in the bad old days and using this recollection as a contrast with their own practices as supervisors now – they describe this deliberate comparison between past and present as 'contrastive rhetoric'. By reflecting on their past using phrases such as 'being left to my own devices', 'you're on your own', ' go away and produce a PhD', 'trial by fire in a weekly seminar', 'he didn't even read what I wrote', 'being thrown in at the deep end', the supervisors were 'vowing' that such things would never happen to their own students.

However, other studies have indicated that certain supervisors model or even mimic their own supervisory approach on their own experience as students. In a nutshell, the attitude is one of 'I will teach as I was taught'. For example, Johnson et al. (2000: 138) describe one supervisor who completed her doctorate in Oxford and reported that the 'Oxford rule' then was that no supervisor should read more than half the thesis. The rationale, reportedly, was that the supervisor wanted the students to be 'quite clear' that the thesis was their own work; this would demonstrate 'the capacity to be autonomous' and to 'work on their own without supervision'. The supervisor now, according to Johnson et al., models her own supervisory practices and approach with Australian students on her past experiences as a student in Oxford.

Johnson et al. (2000) also report reflections of lecturers on their own PhD experience and use terms such as a 'pedagogy of indifference' or 'magisterial disdain' to describe the experiences and the attitudes conveyed in their supervision process. The same paper took (in 2000) a rather gloomy view of the whole supervision relationship by speculating that:

> The experience of isolation and abjection often appears so widespread as to be structural and endemic, a seemingly 'necessary' feature of the doctoral programme for many, rather than an accidental and ameliorable problem. (p. 136)

They go on to discuss whether this situation is perhaps in some senses deliberate, almost a conspiracy, indeed 'a condition of the production of independence and autonomy, which is a goal of the pedagogy and practice of the PhD'. My own view is that is far too gloomy a speculation (and I also argue, in another chapter, that the goal of autonomy is highly problematic anyway. Johnson et al., 2000, themselves argue that the notion of the independent and autonomous scholar is extremely 'gendered').

The question is, of course: will supervisors who have had such negative experiences as students replicate this in their new role, i.e. 'do unto others as was done unto them'? Personally, I have come across a tiny minority of supervisors who adopted this attitude, almost one of 'getting their own back'; this is reminiscent of one of the old arguments used in the debate on corporal punishment in schools: 'well, caning never did me any harm'. Fortunately, I believe this is very much a small minority. Most supervisors whom I have worked with and discussed the issue with feel strongly that if their own doctoral experience was not a positive one they will do their utmost to make the supervision process for their own students a supportive, productive and positive relationship. They deploy the 'contrastive rhetoric' referred to earlier.

My own view is that the supervisors who vowed to do better in Delamont et al.'s study (1998) were engaging in what is now widely known as reflective practice (a term usually attributed to the work of Donald Schön). They were capable of reflecting back on their own doctoral journey and using this reflection to make their own practice supportive and constructive. This concept of reflective practice, or 'meta-supervision' as I termed it earlier, is essential for both supervisor and student to engage in to make the most of the supervision process.

This section has considered some of the issues that can arise with supervisors which students need to be prepared for: the 'I'm so busy' comment; the 'do as was done unto me' approach; supervisors, and sometimes students, not responding in good time … or not at all; not setting deadlines or dates for meetings, again perhaps due to both parties.

The 'not-available' supervisor

Another phenomenon that students need to be aware of is the 'not-available supervisor', rather like the absent landlord. The supervisor, for a range of reasons, is not available for long periods (either face to face or online) and thus the business of arranging meetings, sharing ideas, commenting on written work and communication generally becomes almost impossible. Such absenteeism or lack of availability has been widely reported in the literature – this, and the idea of 'busyness', are discussed by Acker (1999: 82). She reports, and I concur based on my own experience, that such behaviour is regarded by students with 'skepticism and suspicion'. It may occur with 'big name' staff who tread the international stage and are often not available for good reasons – in this case, the 'international expert' may have been the wrong choice of supervisor in the first place and a change (or a new arrangement for co-supervision) may be needed. But I have also seen the situation occur with less eminent staff for a number of reasons: their own work–life balance may be proving difficult; time management is an issue for them; or perhaps the supervision of students may be either a low priority for them or its importance may not be fully rewarded and recognised by the institution they work for. Whatever the cause, it may often result in a supervision arrangement which is simply not right or productive for the student and action needs to be taken by the person in charge of postgraduate work in the department.

The 'too demanding' student

Finally, one other experience I have had as head of research degrees in my department is the supervisor who comes to me and says: 'student X is so demanding'. My first inclination is to think (but not say): 'well, what do you expect, they are paying a hefty fee, you are paid a salary, they want to complete on time and they need guidance and support'. But, having bitten my tongue and explored further, it can sometimes emerge that a student is actually too dependent on help and support from the supervisor(s). This is perhaps the time for the student and supervisor to engage in some 'meta-supervision' and to discuss their respective roles. We have already discussed the idea of autonomy and its nature in work at this level. There is also some discussion in the literature around the connection between concepts of dependency versus autonomy and the importance of gender (for example, Johnson et al., 2000).

Unexpected, unpredictable problems

In a sense, many of the problems and issues discussed already can be predicted or at least are well documented. In this section we look at situations and issues which may arise unexpectedly for students – we follow this with a discussion of a framework for reflecting on them in order to take the right course of action, where possible.

In most cases the issues, problems, worries, doubts or situations which arise can be classified as either procedural or pastoral/social/affective or academic (although in some cases they overlap, e.g. losing your supervisor). We start with academic/cognitive issues.

Academic

These can sometimes involve small differences of view or opinion between student and supervisor – this discrepancy is sometimes called 'dissonance' (e.g. by Wisker et al., 2003). Such differences can occur in discussing and deciding upon, for example:

- *the focus, scope or extent of your project* – in my experience, many students would like to cover a vast area but their supervisor knows this is not possible, manageable or do-able if they are aiming for completion in a finite timescale;
- *the amount of theory* – which theory or theories should be used and why;
- *data collection and data analysis* – most empirical research projects have a tendency towards over-collecting and under-analysing, but sometimes vice versa;

- *dissonance over method* – although fundamental methodological differences between student and supervisor should be anticipated at the outset when choosing supervisor, rifts can sometimes develop and will need careful and sensitive discussion;
- *articulating/linking research questions with methods and methodology, findings, analysis and conclusions* – this is probably the greatest challenge when writing a thesis and should also be one of the key foci for debate and clarification at the viva.

Procedural

Many problems or issues which arise at different phases of the doctoral journey can be classified as procedural although they do overlap with academic and pastoral factors. For example, the time frame and scale of the research project is a procedural matter but does involve academic and social issues. The loss of a supervisor if he or she leaves, retires or suffers long-term illness requires reflection and action (incidentally, supervisors on sabbatical or study leave in most universities are obliged by regulations to continue with their supervision of research degrees students).

In cases of staff loss or illness there are various options. If, for example, your supervisor has moved to another institution (perhaps as a result of 'poaching') then several options are open: first, he or she might be persuaded to carry on supervising you through to completion. This would require not only their willingness and capacity but also the good will and permission of the new employer. The supervisor, or the new employer, may need to be paid to continue working with you but this can often be arranged through your department, e.g. the head of research degrees. The main advantage of this option is the continuity of academic and procedural approach or style; it can also save time, i.e. a new person does not have to pick up the threads or (the bigger risk) change the course of the project to suit their own style and academic preferences.

The second option, if co-supervision is taking place, is for another member of the team to take over; this can often be the best solution. It may then be necessary to bring in another team member but often this can have positive benefits, e.g. fresh enthusiasm, another pair of eyes. The changeover may cause a slight delay but this may be outweighed by the advantages.

Finally, the loss of your supervisor may necessitate finding a new supervisor or a new team perhaps. This should not be the sole responsibility of the student – it is the role of the head of research degrees or head of department to find a replacement as soon as possible who has the workload capacity and the expertise to take over without too much loss of continuity or time. In some departments, particularly small ones, this is unfortunately easier said than done.

Pastoral, social and emotional issues: the affective domain

These can often be the most potent in the course of a research degree – hardly surprisingly as the journey is as much an emotional one as cognitive. Possible problems which might arise are as follows:

- Often, expectations at the start do not match reality – the sheer scale, scope and duration of doctoral study is something that few of us will have experienced before. This can create cognitive 'blocks' as well as affective ones.
- Emotional blocks along the way: students can often have feelings of doubt about their own ability or even their own data – is it good enough? Am I being 'original'? Can I write to the required standard? Can I really work at doctoral level? (We discuss some of these issues in Chapter 6.) Equally guilt pangs, feelings of 'I'm not good enough' and feelings of insecurity can occur at different stages.
- Loneliness and isolation may occur, for example if there is no peer network or critical mass of other students.
- General problems may arise, e.g. time management, life getting in the way, writing blocks, issues of ethics or access.
- Pressures on students to be independent, 'to just go away and get on with it' or not to be 'so demanding', can create anxieties and emotional blocks for many students.
- Balancing roles and juggling balls, e.g. wife/husband, partner, mother/father, carer, may prove difficult.

In many cases, certain of these problems and issues are 'exacerbated for international students' (Wisker et al., 2003: 93; see also Andrade, 2006), for example, due to: the need to face new requirements and a new context, e.g. demands to be 'more critical' and to question assumptions or even 'authority'; over-deference; writing and reviewing which is too descriptive rather than being analytical and critical; the need to take risks; more independent learning, no more spoon feeding; the requirement for in-depth study; the debate on what counts as plagiarism; a new learning environment and approach; and a new social milieu. Many of these situations and demands will not be congruent with their own culture and past learning experiences. But equally, students who are not international will face many of the same challenges and issues when they embark on a postgraduate degree.

Reflecting on and responding to issues and events

How can you respond to these issues, problems and unexpected events as and when they arise? This section presents a possible framework for students and supervisors in trying to understand them and thus attempting to get to grips with them and take action.

The first key factor for a student is to decide how controllable and how pervasive these issues are (Postlethwaite, 1993: 44–5). In plain terms, you should pose these two questions:

- Which issues affect *all* aspects of your work, whatever the context? In contrast, which events and issues affect only **some** aspects of your work, in some contexts?
- Which of the occurrences and issues can be controlled, altered and influenced, i.e. which factors can you and your supervisor actually do something about?

Within these two questions there are two other questions:

- *Internal or external?* If the issue or situation arising can be controlled, altered or influenced is it something internal to you as the student, for example the effort and time you put in? Or is it something external, such as economic status, family problems, bereavement? Is the problem that of the student (or supervisor) or a problem of the context and background?
- *Stable/permanent or unstable/temporary?* Is the issue or barrier something which is constant, unchanging or permanent, or is it short-term or temporary, such as a broken leg, a dose of flu?

These are all questions that should be asked in analysing the factors affecting your doctoral journey and reflecting on your success or failure at certain tasks or activities, e.g. writing up, analysing data, conducting field work.

This basic framework for reflecting on issues and events is summed up in Figure 5.1.

In everyday life, we often do this with ourselves when we consider our own successes and failures and the reasons for them. Is your sheer brilliance due to pure innate ability (internal, stable, not controllable), or is it a result of your drive, motivation and dogged hard work at crucial times (internal, controllable and unstable)? If, like me, you are totally incapable of writing poetry, is it your English teacher's fault because she killed it stone dead for you as a teenager (external, stable and uncontrollable), or is it due to your own lack of creativity and insight (stable, internal and possibly pervasive) (Wellington and Ireson, 2008: 162)?

In a school context, Postlethwaite (1993: 35) explains that 'advantaged pupils' often attribute their own success to internal, stable and pervasive factors such as 'high ability' and those who often fail may attribute that failure to 'low ability' – 'I'm just thick' (internal, stable). They therefore expect to fail again, leading to a downward spiral of self-esteem. Thus the attributions that students make of themselves and those that teachers or supervisors make of them are vitally important in deciding on future action. This is true of students at any level and in particular at postgraduate level. It is hoped that

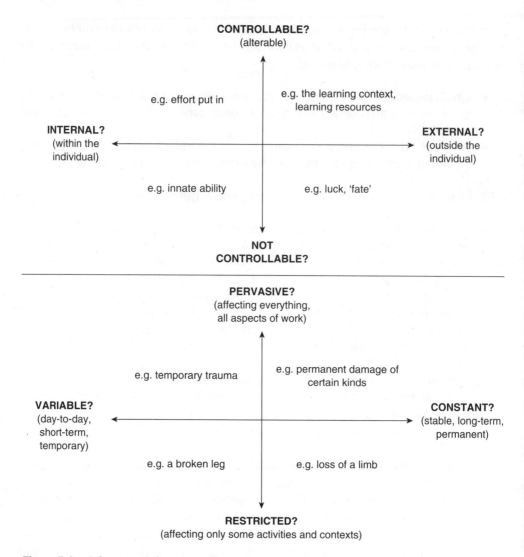

Figure 5.1 A framework for responding to issues and events

the framework in Figure 5.1 will be of value in analysing situations and deciding on future actions.

Past studies of postgraduate failure

In the past, studies have been made into the reasons why postgraduates do not complete their programme. One of the most widely cited is that of Rudd (1985). In many ways, these are still applicable today. I summarise Rudd's main findings (in my own words) below and ask the reader to consider whether these factors are pervasive, controllable, stable, internal or external. Do any of them resonate with your own experiences? Rudd's study found five groups of reasons contributing to failure or success:

1 Qualities and attitudes of the student – e.g. boredom, disenchantment, laziness, lack of motivation or drive, not enjoying it (e.g. if working on a topic imposed upon them).
2 Personal and individual problems – e.g. injury, illness, family problems, change of employment (for part-time students), loneliness.
3 Problems with the research itself – e.g. wrong choice of topic (perhaps too 'large'); wrong choice of university or supervisor; difficulties in gaining access or permissions; failure to achieve results or collect appropriate data.
4 Personal academic problems – e.g. writing problems, feelings of isolation.
5 Problems with supervision – e.g. poor communication, being left to flounder, lack of enthusiasm, not reading drafts after long periods, the supervisor leaving.

We have discussed many of these factors already – it is worth noting that this study, carried out over 25 years ago, identified many issues that will still be present today.

And finally ... the biggest challenge?

In my own experience, often confirmed when talking to supervisors and students, the greatest demand and challenge for a student is to produce, in a well-presented, bound and coherent form, an extended piece of written work. This may seem obvious but the requirement to create an extended piece of writing, ranging from perhaps 45,000 words for some professional doctorates to over 100,000 words in certain areas of the social sciences, is far and away the biggest task in postgraduate work.

This demand can be the main source of doctoral doubts and feelings of inadequacy or insecurity that doctoral students often report. How can these feelings and other barriers to producing such a huge chunk of writing be overcome? We do consider writing the dissertation in Chapter 7 in some detail, but to summarise here there are certain key strategies and attitudes that can be used and developed.

Firstly, avoid perfectionism. Don't try to produce the perfect draft at the first time of asking, certainly, but also bear in mind that perfectionism is unattainable for most mortals, even in the tenth draft. As Becker (1998) helpfully says: 'don't get it right, get it written'.

Second, start writing from day one of the journey. You may well look back on this writing when two years have elapsed and decide not to keep it – but at least your thoughts and ideas have been recorded and left a few footprints.

Third – and this is easier said than done – try to avoid distractions and displacements. These might be the urgent need to answer your e-mails or more subtly, in my experience, a constantly felt need to keep reading. At some point, you have to stop reading and start writing – preferably do the two side by side (as one of my students put it, it helps if every time you read something, your write something).

Fourthly, break a writing task into manageable, do-able chunks so that your goals are shorter and more realisable.

And finally, never underestimate the time it takes to produce a piece of writing. I have authored or co-authored 12 books now and it still takes longer to write a chapter (or a paragraph) than I expect.

In conclusion ...

> The supervisory process is certainly complex, pivotal, crucial, responsible and important ... but it remains elusive, mysterious and ambiguous as well. (Acker, 1999: 91)

This chapter has looked at some of the complexities of the supervision process, the obstacles and aids that can help or hinder the doctoral journey, the responsibilities on both sides and some ideas for reflecting on them and taking action. We have discussed possible crises of confidence and doctoral doubts and have taken a positive view of how possible problems and issues can be prevented or, at worst, cured.

One of the key messages of the chapter is the vital importance of the affective domain and the need for supervisors to encourage, motivate, cajole and coach at different times. Achieving a postgraduate degree is more than purely a cognitive matter.

 Further reading

Denicolo, P. and Pope, M. (1994) 'The postgraduate's journey: interplay of roles', in O. Zuber-Skerritt and Y. Ryan (eds), *Quality in Postgraduate Education*. London: Kogan Page.

Johnson, L., Lee, A. and Green, B. (2000) 'The PhD and the autonomous self: gender, rationality, and postgraduate pedagogy', *Studies in Higher Education*, 25: 135–47.

6

The ultimate goal: achieving a doctorate

 Chapter aims

In this chapter we examine the key features and purposes of the doctorate, with a view to better understanding the supervision process and the way that doctorates are assessed.

The chapter considers some of the big issues for students embarking on and undertaking a research degree and for those supervising and examining them, for example:

- What is the purpose of a doctorate? What are they for?
- What is 'doctorateness'? How do supervisors and students see it?
- What is *theory* in the PhD and the professional doctorate?
- What is meant by 'originality'?

Introduction

There has always been something dynamic and evolving about the doctorate and its nature. This has occurred across time, as we saw in Chapter 2: from the early medieval idea of a 'licence to teach' through to its more Humboldtian conception as a research degree in Germany, and now to the current era of auditing, accountability, quality assurance and regulation. The doctorate can also be seen in different forms across the world (Powell and Green, 2007). As a result, the notion of a doctorate varies across space and across different disciplines. In the current context, the doctorate is characterised by diversity (as we saw in earlier chapters). Thus variability, both historically and geographically, is probably the key to understanding the doctorate. This variability makes the search for some sort of inner essence to the doctorate rather like the hunt for the Holy Grail.

In practice, the answer to the question 'what is a doctorate?' depends to a large extent on who is asking, as well as when and where the question is being asked. For example, in this era of accountability, there is a wide range of stakeholders posing the question – these stakeholders include the student, supervisors, examiners, academics generally, other professionals and, increasingly, employers.

What is the purpose of a doctorate?

One way of looking at 'doctorateness' and what it means is to take a teleological approach, i.e. to consider what it is for – what is its purpose?

Personal goals

If you asked a range of postgraduate students why they had embarked on a doctoral programme, you would be certain to receive a wide range of responses (including, perhaps, a cynical shrug and a comment of 'I really don't know' if you asked that student at the wrong moment). My own research with a colleague (see Wellington and Sikes, 2006, for a full discussion) has revealed that students have a vast range of motivations for undertaking a doctorate. Some reasons may be *intrinsic* and very personal, for example: 'I wanted to prove to myself that I could reach the highest level'. Intrinsic motivations can also relate to personal curiosity and interest or the challenge that doctoral work poses. Equally, motivations can be *extrinsic* and related to factors outside of the student's intrinsic desires and goals. For example, some see it as a ticket to either a job or to promotion if they are already employed; some see it as a means to improve their kudos and standing, perhaps in their own work setting or even their home context.

Process versus products

Another, closely related, way of reflecting on the teleology of the doctorate is to consider its purposes in terms of *outsiders* and their interests in it. These purposes could include the following:

1 It could be regarded as preparation for a future role or a future career. For example, the doctorate might be seen as producing the next batch of researchers, it might be seen as an academic apprenticeship or it might still be seen as a licence to teach (in higher education). Equally – and this is especially true in the present context – it might be seen as preparation for industry or other employment.

2 Those already working might see it as career development or continuing professional development (CPD), or it might be seen as a way of researching one's own practice with a view to improving it. (This is especially true of students undertaking a part-time PhD or a professional doctorate.)

3 Some outsiders might regard a doctorate as a vehicle for a person to develop certain generic skills which might then be transferable to other contexts, not least employment. These skills might include problem-solving, researching, writing and communicating; they might be grouped together in a cluster that some like to call 'employability'. This call for the development of generic skills has increased since the Roberts Review of 2002 – it is a highly debated and contested area, raising such questions as: are such skills genuinely transferable or are they necessarily embedded in a context? Can they be learnt or 'inculcated' out of context? Is the acquisition of these skills a distraction from the main purpose of achieving a doctorate?

4 The doctorate could be seen largely in terms of a student's personal development and her/his achievement; or it might be seen as nothing to do with the outcomes listed above, but in terms of satisfying someone's personal and deeply felt curiosity and intellectual interest in an area or a need to prove oneself. (A study by Leonard et al., 2005, showed that this is surprisingly common.)

5 Finally, the purpose of the doctorate might be seen in terms of its product, for example: knowledge production; pushing forward the boundaries of knowledge; adding new or 'original' knowledge; creating a novel position (i.e. a thesis) on an area of research; the generation of knowledge which can be transferred – to industry, perhaps, or at least to be disseminated.

The five potential purposes above relate to a useful distinction when considering the nature of a doctorate – and the supervision process. Is it largely about **process,** i.e. personal development, preparing a person for a career, inculcating certain transferable skills, giving personal satisfaction and pride? Or is the doctorate mainly concerned with its **product,** i.e. a body of knowledge, adding to existing work?

This could be seen as a tension between process and product. In reality, the supervision process should be concerned with both. It is important, during supervision, for everyone involved to reflect on the purposes of this particular doctorate and the motivation behind it. What is the doctorate for, in your case? Is it primarily to develop the person, in which case the process is uppermost? Or is it about knowledge production, the 'thesis' and the addition of 'original' knowledge? To what extent are the twin demands of process and product in balance? Should student and supervisor attempt to balance them?

This question is particularly relevant when it comes to the examination process for the doctorate, i.e. the written dissertation and the oral examination, the viva voce. In the viva (which we examine in detail in Chapter 10) there really should be questions about both areas: to what extent was the doctoral journey a vehicle for your personal development, learning and growth? What skills did you acquire during the course of the research? To what extent is it a contribution to the body of knowledge in an area of study?

So ... just what is a doctorate?

**What sort of a question is that? Why is it
difficult to get a straight answer to this question?**

The first thing to consider is what kind of a question is being asked here. What questions is it like? Is it like asking: what does it mean to be British? What does it mean to be human? Is it more like the question: what is an animal or what is a plant?

So, for example, by asking it are we searching for some sort of inner, essential quality that characterises 'doctorateness' (like 'human-ness' or 'British-ness')? My own view is that to search for a single, common meaning belonging to all doctorates is rather like looking for the Holy Grail – our chances of success are quite slim. No, my view is that doctorates have certain 'family resemblances' which link them together rather than some inner, core meaning. The concept of family resemblances is taken from Wittgenstein's later thinking (in *Philosophical Investigations)* in which he discusses the nature of concepts and what makes them (in my words) hang together. He uses the example of games and the concept of a game. Consider a wide spectrum of examples of games: dominoes, chess, hopscotch, football, cricket, tiddlywinks, PlayStation games and *Trivial Pursuit* (these are my examples, not his). Do they all have certain characteristics in common? Well, some might, e.g. cricket and football both have eleven players in a team and they use a ball. But others do not. Games have what Wittgenstein called a 'family resemblance'. As a result of these resemblances, we can recognise a game when we see one (so if we went to a new country and saw two people pushing plastic tokens around on a board we might ask: 'what's their game'). But we would find it hard to define 'game'.

My view is that doctorateness is rather like this. Examiners have said to me that 'they know a doctorate when they see one'. However, I do think that we owe it to students to go a bit further than this and remove some of the mystique – to try to make explicit some of the descriptions and characteristics that might appear tacit and implicit.

Giving some reality to the question: making it 'operational'

We can do this by observing – and asking about – what examiners actually say and do **in practice**. Clearly, the two embodiments in reality of a doctorate are the written dissertation and then the viva voce, the oral examination. These are the two ways in which the doctorate becomes real or tangible (or at least audible): the written *dissertation* (which contains the student's thesis or position); and the *viva voce*, the oral examination.

Can we begin to unpack or unpick what a doctorate is by considering these two realisations of it? My answer is yes, and we can look at it from two perspectives (at least) – the examiner and the examinee. What do they say about it? What do examiners say makes a good thesis? What do examiners actually want from, and look for in, a dissertation? How do different examiners approach the viva? What are students actually asked in the viva?

We examine the examiner's view of what makes a good thesis in Chapters 7 and 9; in Chapter 10 we look in detail at the viva, how examiners approach it and the kinds of questions that tend to be asked.

'Doctorateness': what do written regulations say?

Here we look at one very important way in which we can explore how people perceive and articulate 'doctorateness': by looking at written regulations. All universities which offer and therefore examine research degrees will have documents with titles beginning with phrases such as: 'Guidelines for examiners of candidates for ...'; 'Notes for the guidance of research students, supervisors and examiners ...'; 'Notes on examination procedures for ...'; 'Guide to examiners ...'; 'Regulations for degrees of ...'; or 'Examination of the thesis: notes for examiners'. Having been external examiner for research degrees at a number of these institutions I have collected (sad character that I am) an extensive sample of such documents. It is a valuable exercise to pick out some of the key terms, criteria and descriptors that are written in them. (I will also do this in the chapter of this book on the viva, its purpose and conduct – and the discussion of the various recommendations which examiners can make after the oral examination.)

Here is a sample of some of the key phrases and expressions relating to doctorateness:

- Addition to knowledge
- Worthy of publication either in full or abridged form
- Presents a thesis embodying the results of the research
- Original work which forms an addition to knowledge
- Makes a distinct contribution to the knowledge of the subject and offers evidence of originality shown by the discovery of new facts and/or the exercise of independent critical power
- Shows evidence of systematic study and the ability to relate the results of such study to the general body of knowledge in the subject
- The thesis should be a demonstrably coherent body of work
- Shows evidence of adequate industry and application
- Has taken account of previously published work on the subject
- Understands the relationship of the special theme of the thesis to a wider field of knowledge
- Represents a significant contribution to learning, for example through the discovery of new knowledge, the connection of previously unrelated facts, the development of new theory or the revision of older views
- Provides originality and independent critical ability and must contain matter suitable for publication
- Independent critical ability
- Original work
- Adequate knowledge of the field of study
- Competence in appropriate methods of performance and recording of research
- Ability in style and presentation
- Is clearly written
- Takes account of previously published work on the subject

'Doctorateness': the supervisor's perspective

We have seen some of the written regulations which attempt to make explicit what a doctorate should be. What do individuals say? When I interviewed experienced supervisors and examiners for this book, very personal perspectives were expressed on the nature of the doctorate. One interviewee was at first reluctant to go beyond intuition:

You know it when you see it – often I've seen Masters work that I've thought is doctoral level. It's intuitive and tacit.

But this supervisor then went on to say:

> They've got to show evidence of critical reflection – it's about **not** taking things for granted and questioning assumptions ... and good writing is increasingly important for me as a criterion for 'doctorateness'; you should be communicating your knowledge clearly.

Another supervisor, also an experienced examiner, felt that a doctoral student is an 'apprentice' but that this notion may be different in the professional doctorate:

> It's an apprenticeship in doing research, in the social sciences anyway. Somebody is going on a journey, even in a professional doctorate – although this is a more restricted form, it's more tightly bounded. They are a different sort of apprentice, they need even more supervision. Some find it difficult to really engage with the fact that this is a piece of research, they start by seeing it more as a professional report ... and that makes it quite difficult to shape it.

Finally, a third supervisor, when asked what a doctorate is told me:

> I could trot out the usual responses but I actually think it's more than that – in my area, it's a huge journey, a journey that you've no idea what you face when you start. It's a hugely challenging personal journey which brings into relief sometimes many issues that you thought you could leave behind but can't ...

'Doctorateness' and doing a doctorate: the student's perspective

I would guess that there are as many student views on what a doctorate is as there are students. I only quote two of my student interviewees here, as illustrations. Interestingly, for both, the doctorate is a very personal matter which ties in with much of the previous literature on students' motivations and perceptions (e.g. Leonard et al., 2005; Wellington and Sikes, 2006):

> It means that you're really clever – for me, it's a way of proving to myself that I must be clever, because I never feel it. Somehow this certificate will prove it. But the other thing is that I love my subject – I want to show that I've got a deep knowledge of my subject and I could be called an 'expert' on it.

> Its intrinsic worth is the main thing for me. It's such a gift to be able to spend three years or more doing something that you absolutely love, and it's your job to be passionately interested in it. I'm enjoying doing it because it's such an opportunity. It means so much to me because it's such a privilege to be able to do it.

When I asked the same students their views on the criteria for 'doctorateness' they said:

> That you can argue a case and that your argument is supported by rigorous research and evidence, without any flaws (or huge flaws anyway). It's rather like Law, when you present the case for and against something.

> If other people read it, it changes their thinking, it gets them to think differently, to see things in a different way ... even if it's just for that moment when they're reading it ... to expand people's perceptions and the way they see things.

The place of theory in achieving 'doctorateness'

> There is nothing so practical as a good theory. *(Lewin, 1951: 169)*

A continuing debate relating to postgraduate work, especially in the social sciences, has concerned the status, the purpose and the function of theory. What is its place in the doctorate? Is the presence of theory an essential criterion for doctorateness? These large questions in turn raise more specific ones: where should theory come into your study? Should it be the main guiding force, determining the study and its methodology from the outset – or should it emerge from the study? Can certain forms of empirical work be conducted without prior theory (in this sense, prior conceptions and theories are said to be bracketed or put to one side)? Or is all research, and all observation, 'theory-laden', as Karl Popper termed it?

The matter is complicated for students (and supervisors), of course, by lack of agreement over what theory actually is. The issue is complex but it is an important one for anyone involved in undertaking and supervising research. The discussion of 'theory' is more than a theoretical matter – it is of great practical importance in determining an external examiner's judgement of a dissertation or an oral examination, the *viva voce*. For example, students are sometimes accused of lacking a theoretical framework or a theory base to their work.

Practical outcomes of this accusation could be the requirement to make amendments to or resubmit a thesis – or could even lead to the non-award of a higher degree. Or, at the next stage, it might lead to the rejection by a referee of an article submitted for publication. In short, being accused of lacking a theoretical base or, even worse, of being 'a-theoretical' can be practically very serious.

What is 'theory'?

Like most problematic words, 'theory' does not lend itself to easy definition – and worse, we cannot always recognise one when we see one. The *Oxford*

English Dictionary shows that the word originates from the ancient Greek idea of a 'theor', a person who acts as a spectator or an envoy, perhaps sent on behalf of a state to consult an oracle. More recently, the word theory was taken to mean a mental view or a conception, or a system of ideas used for explanation of a group of facts or phenomena (dated 1638 in the *Oxford English Dictionary*).

In the physical sciences, the distinction between phenomena/events (i.e. things which happen), laws and theories is relatively clear. A *law* is a statement telling us *what* happens in terms of a general pattern or rule. If a metal rod is heated it expands; if pressure is exerted on a gas in a container, its volume decreases (Boyle's Law); every action has an equal and opposite reaction (Newton's Third Law). Laws are simply statements of patterns or connections. For this reason they are less tentative and more long-lasting than theories. The law 'When a gas is heated it expands' (Charles' Law) will be true two centuries from now. But the theories used to encompass or support laws are more tentative.

Theories are used to explain *why* specific events and patterns of events occur as they do. As such, they are explanations constructed by human beings and therefore subject to improvement, refinement and sometimes rejection, i.e. they are tentative.

What has this discussion to do with a student undertaking postgraduate research? Quite simply, a student will not be awarded a doctorate unless she or he has considered the place of theory in their thesis. It is an essential element. Theory can play a part in four ways. Firstly, theories are used to explain *why* things happen. They *are* tentative, but not that tentative (Newton was born over 300 years ago and his theories still have widespread applicability and practical value, e.g. in building bridges, getting to the Moon and back). Secondly, theories are a way of *seeing things*. They often involve models or metaphors which help us to visualise or understand events, e.g. the atom is 'rather like' the Solar System. Thirdly, the existence of an established theory (certainly in science but more debatably in social research) can shape or determine the way we subsequently 'see' things. In short, observation is often *theory-laden*. The theory determines the observation. Finally, it needs to be noted that an established theory can *predict* as well as explain, i.e. theories may be predictive as well as explanatory. The particle theory of matter can be used not only to explain what happens to matter, e.g. phenomena like melting or boiling, but also what *will* happen in new situations (e.g. if impurities are added, how boiling will be affected).

Theories, models and metaphors in social research

The role of theory in social research, just like in the physical sciences, is to help us to understand events and to see them in a new or a different way. A theory may be a metaphor, a model or a framework for understanding or making sense of social events. Other elements in social research which are sometimes (often unjustifiably) given the name 'theory' are little more than generalisations, alleged patterns, ideas or even simply labels.

The view I have argued for elsewhere (Wellington and Szczerbinski, 2008: 39) is that a theory in social research is only worthy of the name if it helps us to *explain* phenomena and thereby aid our understanding of it. It provides a new way of seeing things. A theory may also have *predictive* power as well as explanatory value, although this may be expecting too much in social research.

Metaphors and models often fulfil at least the first criterion. A model is basically a simplification of reality – it simplifies and aids our understanding by concentrating on certain features of a phenomenon while ignoring others. A classic case is the world-renowned map of the London Underground – a simplification or idealisation of a messy, complicated system. But the model or map we use serves its purpose. An example of a model from learning theory is Vygotsky's idea of a 'zone of proximal development': this is a model which talks about a zone between what a learner already knows or can do and what the learner can potentially do with help from a teacher.

Metaphors are like bridges (the word 'metaphor' literally means 'carry over' or 'carry across') which link the unknown or the unfamiliar to the known or familiar. A metaphor in learning is Bruner's notion of 'scaffolding' – this is the idea that a student's learning can be brought on or built up by using support or scaffolding to move the learner to a new level. It is a useful metaphor for teachers at all levels, provided it is used with care and not taken too far.

When does theory come in: before (a priori)? Or after (a posteriori)?

The key question for students engaged in, or about to embark on, research is not *whether* theory should make its entry but *when*.

- Should theory be brought in prior to the research in order to guide it and make observation theory-laden, i.e. a priori?
- Or should theory emerge from data collection and observation and be developed from it, i.e. inductively, a posteriori? (This approach is often called 'grounded theory'.)

The simple answer to these complex questions is: it depends totally on the nature of your research, its purpose and the area being investigated. In some fields there are ample theories, so sufficiently well developed that it would be wrong not to use them in shaping research design and data collection. In others, there may be a shortage of suitable theory, or it may be extremely tentative, thus implying a different approach. Similarly with the purpose of a research project – a key aim of a project may be to *replicate* previous research in order to lend support to a theory or perhaps to attempt to refine it. In others, the aim may be to develop new, tentative theories which (perhaps) subsequent researchers might build on.

Whichever way you and your supervisor(s) view theory and its place in the dissertation, consideration of it is an essential feature of work at postgraduate level.

This difficult word: originality

The word 'originality' – like many words, including 'criticality' – is one which is widely used in this context but (again like many) has a range of meanings, few of which are shared perhaps.

The key question for this section is: ***what forms can an 'original contribution' take in a doctoral thesis?*** A range of authors have written on this – I attempt below to provide my own summary of the different meanings given to the term 'originality' in regulations, handbooks, documents, discussions and vivas. I have grouped them, arbitrarily, into eight categories:

1   Building new knowledge: wall metaphors:
    - building on or extending previous work
    - putting a new brick in the wall
    - plugging a perceived gap in the wall
      (Demolishing an old wall and/or rebuilding a new one would count as a paradigm shift. Nobody expects a paradigm shift for a doctorate, unless it's Wittgenstein's – or Einstein's, and he never did one.)

2   Original processes or approaches:
    - new methods or techniques applied to an existing area of study
    - new methods or techniques applied to a new area
    - using a proven technique/approach/methodology but in a new area
    - using a new mixture of methods
    - refinement and improvement of methods applied to existing or new areas of study
    - cross-disciplinary approach to an existing area or a new area
    - testing someone else's ideas/concepts/theories in the 'field', i.e. new empirical work 'testing' or illuminating existing theory

3   New syntheses:
    - of methods or methodologies (see 2 above)
    - connecting previous studies

- connecting/linking/juxtaposing existing theories to make a new compound
- linking two or more previous thinkers

4 New charting or mapping of territory:
   - exploring a new territory
   - discovering a new territory
   - refining an earlier exploration
   - re-charting a territory
   - opening up new areas (e.g. that were taboo) or neglected areas
   - 'clearing the undergrowth' (John Locke, English philosopher) to make way for further thinking or empirical work

5 New implications:
   - for practice and practitioners
   - for policy and policy-makers
   - for theory and theorists

6 Revisiting a recurrent issue or debate – bringing one or more of these to bear on an old chestnut or a recurrent issue, e.g. class size:
   - new evidence
   - new thinking
   - new theory

7 Replicating or reproducing existing work:
   - place: replicating work from elsewhere in a new geographical context, e.g. a study carried out in South East Asia replicated in the UK
   - time: replicating in a new time context, e.g. work in the 1990s revisited in 2010
   - reproducing or replicating existing work with a different sample, e.g. a new age group, a larger sample

8 New presentation – new ways of writing, presenting, disseminating

Personal views on 'originality'

The above list of eight categories in which people may be 'original' is intended to be useful in thinking about your own work. But the final word on this topic comes from one supervisor and one student, who both expressed in their own way the view that the notion of originality is a problematic one.

From the supervisor's perspective

Originality? I think a lot of students are put off by that word. They think 'well, I'm not going to discover penicillin' or I'm not going to be able to do these things. But once they realise that it's their study, then the originality itself will be in there ... and they've got to draw it out. If the student and the supervisors have done their jobs together, that originality should be there anyway, it should emerge from the study. It needn't be about a substantive issue, it may be about methodology, or often both.

From a student's perspective

I think it's actually different for medical research when you make a break-through and the treatment of x, y or z will never be the same again because of this particular breakthrough ... but when you're dealing with ideas ... it is kind of unlikely that one person will have a totally new idea. There's something in the ether about ways of thinking that everyone picks up on and we all start to think in those ways anyway. Subtle influences all around – we live in a cultural milieu, with centuries of thinking. You can't separate yourself out from that. Who knows where all your 'influences' come from? It depends on the context you are in (time and space).

Further tensions and debates around the doctorate

In Chapter 2 we listed some of the key issues around the nature and purpose of the doctorate that have been recurring over its history. I would like to finish this chapter by highlighting three 'tensions' that need to be discussed by student and supervisor in reflecting upon their particular study and their unique dissertation:

- Is it aimed primarily at taking theory forward ... or to utilise theory in a new way ... to apply theory to a real situation ... or should postgraduate research primarily have **utility value**, i.e. to be of practical use in a situation, a profession or an industry?
- Should the focus be on **process** (researcher/personal development) ... or on **product** (adding to the corpus of knowledge/transferring knowledge)?
- Should the emphasis be on completing in time ...? or on producing quality, no matter how long it takes?

In conclusion ...

This chapter has looked in some detail at the key questions which underpin the idea of 'doctorateness' and the regulations and actual practices which translate this into reality for the doctoral student. I have tried to do this by examining the purposes of doctorates for different people, by looking at the role of theory in a thesis, by summarising the various meanings of 'originality' which seem to be held and by listing the tensions that still lurk behind discussions about the doctorate.

My own view is that when it comes to judgements on and decisions about a thesis, the usual '-itys' are all worth bearing in mind: originality, publishability and criticality. But certainly the first and last are contested: what does it mean to be critical? What are the criteria for it? How does it show itself, i.e. how is it realised in practice? This, like originality and 'doctorateness' itself, is often left undiscussed and kept tacit or implicit. The key things are how these '-itys' pan out in reality, i.e. in the written thesis and the viva, *and* how the examiners judge whether they are present in the written and oral parts of the examination. By their deeds they shall be known – not by the written regulations of the university they are examining in, either as externals or internals. How do they interpret these criteria and judge their presence or absence?

The key word is **contribution**, without the complication of the adjective 'original' or even publishable. The key criteria would then be: does the doctoral dissertation (and its live version, the viva voce) have a thesis in the sense of a position and an argument? Has the thesis made a contribution to the field of study? Has it built on previous arguments and theses (from previous literature) and pushed it forward a little or added to it? Does it provide another brick in the wall? Will this contribution potentially make an impact – or bring about a change – in thinking and to theory, policy or practice?

 **Further reading**

Park, C. (2007) *Redefining the Doctorate*. York: Higher Education Academy.

Phillips, E. and Pugh, D. (2000) *How to Get a PhD*, 3rd edn. Buckingham: Open University Press.

Taylor, S. and Beasley, N. (2005) *A Handbook for Doctoral Supervisors*. London: RoutledgeFalmer.

Tinkler, P. and Jackson, C. (2004) *The Doctoral Examination Process: A Handbook for Students, Examiners and Supervisors*. Maidenhead: SRHE/Open University Press.

7

Getting the thesis written

Chapter aims

This chapter focuses on the important business of actually producing your written dissertation and the part that the supervision process should play in this. The chapter considers:

- writing and the writing process;
- the affective domain and writing;
- what supervisors and students should expect from each other when it comes to the business of writing;
- working successfully with your supervisor;
- guidance on writing which can help in the supervision process;
- keeping your own identity and voice – a delicate balance.

The issue of 'what makes a good thesis?' is a question which we follow up in Chapter 9.

Introduction

As argued in Chapter 5, the biggest single task and the greatest challenge in completing a postgraduate degree of any kind is to produce a written dissertation. The length of this may vary from around 45,000 words for some professional doctorates (which usually follows the successful completion of several substantial, assessed assignments) to over 100,000 words for some

PhDs, especially if they contain large amounts of qualitative data. This not only involves a huge of amount of industry and energy (not least in the actual physical completion of a well presented, carefully paginated and neatly bound product) but it also requires a considerable intellectual effort to produce a critical, cogent and coherent body of writing, based on a wide range of literature and offering some form of original contribution. The aim of this chapter is to discuss how this can be achieved with the help of your supervisor, and some of the useful guidance which is at hand on the production of a written thesis.

Writing and the writing process

Writing as a way of thinking

The traditional, popular model of writing was based on the idea that 'what you want to say and how you say it in words are two quite separate matters' (Thomas, 1987). Others have called it the 'think and then write paradigm' (Moxley, 1997: 6), i.e. we do all of our thinking before we start writing. Writers first decide what they want to say and then choose the words to express their thoughts and their meaning, i.e. you decide what you want to say, and then you write it down.

Thomas (1987: 95–8) analyses several ways in which a belief in this classical model can be harmful, or 'lead to trouble' as he puts it. First, belief in the model creates the expectation that writing should be easy if 'you know your stuff'. Then, when people find it difficult (as we all do) feelings of inadequacy and frustration set in. Second, the model leads to the incorrect belief that thorough knowledge will lead to clear, high-quality writing. This is not always true and can again lead to negative feelings. Third, the expectation that writing is a linear process can lead to feelings of inadequacy and frustration as soon as the writer realises that it is in fact recursive or cyclical. Finally, the classic model goes something like: do all your reading, grasp your entire material, think it through, plan it out and then write. Writers who follow this would never get started.

In reality, thinking and writing interact. This should be the basic premise on which the supervision process is founded, i.e. thinking occurs during writing, *as* we write, not before it. Elbow (1981) described this model, the generative model, as involving two processes: growing and cooking. Writing various drafts and getting them on paper is growing; rereading them, asking for comments from others and revising is part of the cooking process. Adopting and believing in this model will lead to several important attitudes and strategies which all contribute to a more valuable supervision process:

- greater willingness to revise one's writing (drafting and redrafting);
- a willingness to postpone the sequencing and planning of one's writing until one is into the writing process (it is easier to arrange and structure ideas and words once they are out there on paper, than in our heads);
- a habit of 'write first, edit later';
- the attitude that extensive revisions to a piece of writing are a strength not a weakness;
- more willingness to ask for comment and feedback and to take this on board;
- greater sensitivity to readers and their needs, prior experience and knowledge and their reasons for reading it.

By adopting this model, the process of supervision and the benefits from it, are greatly enhanced.

So the argument in this section is simple: writing is a form of thinking. It is not something that follows thought but goes along in tandem with it. Laurel Richardson (1990 and 1998) often describes writing as a way of 'knowing', a method of *discovery* and analysis. Becker (1986: 17) puts it beautifully by saying: 'The first draft is for discovery, not for presentation'. This process of learning, discovery and analysis does not precede the writing process – it is part of it.

In contrast, if supervision is based on the traditional model of writing, this can undermine people's confidence and act as a block or obstacle in getting started on a piece of writing. If we feel that we can't start until we know exactly what we think, what we intend to write and how we are going to organise it, then we will never get started. This is one of the reasons why Richardson objects to the term 'writing up' of research, as if it comes afterwards. Like the linear model of writing, this is based on a similarly false model of the research process as being linear, which puts 'writing up' as the last task (see later in this chapter and also Wellington, 2000: 46–9).

Planning, thinking and writing

The view that writing is a form of thinking does not rule out the need for planning. Plans are a starting point for writers. Although a few writers follow them meticulously most treat the plan as something to deviate from.

Here are some of the points made by experienced authors whom I interviewed for a book entitled *Getting Published* (all extracts taken from Wellington, 2003: Chapter 3):

I like to write to a plan. I produce section headings and fairly detailed jottings about what these will contain and then follow them through. Sometimes I find that the plan isn't working so I revise it – I never write without an outline to my side though.

I do plan my writing but I usually find that in the process of writing the plan might take a new direction. I will then 'go with the flow'.

I have ideas in the back of my mind but I only really know what I want to say as I begin to write things down. I rarely write the proper introduction until I have finished.

I usually pre-plan it, though on the occasions when I've just let it 'flow' it seems to have worked quite well. The more sure I am of the theme the more natural it would be to let it flow, at least on first draft. I think I do a lot of thinking beforehand but invariably the act of writing is creative for me – some new links and strands pop up. I think I do structure my writing though the structure often gets revised.

I put a lot of emphasis on pre-planning and particularly on structure, because the nature of what I write is argumentative. So I need the structure of the argument mapped out – and I work to this map. But quite often I don't actually, myself, understand fully what the argument is until I've done the first draft. So the first draft is a learning curve.

I plan things visually, with a spidergram. I brainstorm ideas then try to connect them with a spidergram or a mind map. I find that as I'm writing the plan changes. If I write under subheadings it's easier to move things. I can cut and paste, or move things to the bottom of the page if I don't know where to put them.

These comments show that different people adopt different approaches to planning and even that the same writers sometimes use different approaches. Planning is an important activity for all writers. The extent and style of the planning seems to vary from one to another but all plan in some way. Some writers plan in a very visual way by using mind mapping or spidergrams and use metaphors such as sketching the landscape, taking a route or forming a map. Others seem to plan in a more verbal way.

Writing is seen as a learning process by most authors. They talk of learning through their writing, as opposed to writing activity occurring as a result of their learning. Again, this is an important point for the supervision process – if both parties treat writing as a form of thinking and a way of learning the process will be more beneficial and also less likely to create tension and anxiety.

Writing is difficult

One of the reasons why some students become frustrated with their writing is that they forget how difficult writing is (for most people). It is also an experience that has an emotional side to it – writing involves feelings such as pain, pleasure, frustration, enjoyment, relief, stress, angst and satisfaction, in varying quantities and at different times. It is vital that the 'feelings' side of writing is borne in mind by both supervisor and student. Writing is more than just a cognitive process.

Perhaps the main thing to remember about writing is that it is hard, even painful, work. It is a struggle. Writing clearly and succinctly is even more difficult. Having extensive experience of writing does not make it easier, it simply makes the writer more confident. My own interviews with different writers, many of them experienced and widely published, is that they all face barriers to writing – and the 'aids' they use to overcome so-called writers' block can be quite creative! (Again, these comments are taken from Wellington, 2003: Chapter 3):

> I get it all the time and I don't deal with it. I just stay there and plug away. I have to have total silence else I can't think. I do sometimes go and stand in the shower for 15 minutes or so and I find that can make me feel better.

> If I get stuck I reread what I have already produced and often spend a bit of time rephrasing things or clarifying. This usually helps me get in the frame of mind for writing and I can then continue by building on the writing already there. If that is no help I might read for a while and this may give me a few ideas on how to get going or I might draw diagrams. I use the diagrams to set out my ideas in a different way than words and this might then help to clarify what I am trying to do.

> I don't know where to go next. Sometimes I just give up and do something else. Other times I go back to another chapter or a different subheading, or even my spidergram. Other times I just try to write my way through it, knowing that I'll probably delete most of it.

Different writers like to work at different times of the day, under different conditions and have different routines and avoidance strategies:

> I find procrastination to be a useless but common avoidance strategy. I write (and do most things) best in the morning and would regard 9–1 as being optimum writing time. I tend to leave routine chores (referencing, etc.) for late afternoon.

> I need silence, no noise at all. I write at the desk in my study, with the desk cleared of clutter. I write best in the morning between 8 and 1. A round-the-block or to-the-newsagents walk for 10 minutes helps enormously.

> I had a colleague once who said: 'If I don't write in the morning, I can't write all day' … and I really relate to that. There can be days on end where I just sort of go back and only move forward a sentence at a time. I find it's

best just to leave it and do something else. Often if you do leave it, you find that something happens, out of the blue, that suddenly gives a different perspective on what you were writing about ... and you can come back and start again. I suppose it's the subconscious working on things – it leaves the mind open.

Many people feel the need for incubation, for lying fallow or for mulling things over during the business of writing something – especially during a long piece of work such as a doctoral thesis or a chapter in a thesis. Again, this is something that students and supervisors need to bear in mind during the doctoral journey.

Feelings and emotions in writing: the affective domain

The idea of an affective domain

It is clear from some of the voices in the previous section that there is more to writing than simply skill, knowledge and ability. This is an important part of writing but writing, and receiving feedback on it, are **emotional** experiences. The feelings and emotions in any learning process are part of what Bloom (1956) called the affective domain. The affective domain is the component which involves the feeling and emotional side of learning and teaching, i.e. enjoyment, motivation, drive, passion enthusiasm, inspiration. The work of Bloom and others has had something of a revival in the last few years, and more attention is now being paid to the affective domain in the area of student writing (for example, Lillis, 2001). Writing involves a great deal of cognitive energy. But for most if not all people, writing is also an experience that involves strong feelings and emotions: pain, pleasure, frustration, enjoyment, angst, annoyance, relief and stress. The affective domain in writing is important and is therefore worth exploring and discussing, especially during supervision sessions, with the aim of helping people to recognise it, to 'deal with it' and even to improve their writing by doing so.

Most doctoral students will have both positive and negative feelings about writing. For example, some of the positive attitudes towards writing that I have come across include:

- 'Writing helps me to make sense of my ideas.'
- 'It helps to clarify and organise my thoughts.'
- 'It's exciting and helps me to think.'
- 'It's rewarding; it gives me a feeling of being productive.'

But equally, some of the negative attitudes and comments on writing that have been expressed to me include:

- 'It's painstaking – I have lots of stuff in my head and I can't put it into words.'
- 'I always worry about getting started.'
- 'Knowing there is an audience for it can be intimidating.'

Students also talk about writing being daunting, stressful or even torture.

Everyone who writes will have positive and negative feelings about writing, a kind of love–hate relationship. Doctoral students are no exception. These are well worth exploring and sharing either with your peers or your supervisor or both. Simply knowing that writing is hard work for most people can be quite consoling.

Factors which make matters worse

Two views on, or models of, writing can make matters worse. The first is the model of writing mentioned earlier, which suggests that we do all our thinking and then we write our thoughts on paper or screen. This model is held by some students with comments such as: 'I feel as if I need to know everything first'. The second factor which is a common inhibitor is the fear of an audience. Knowing that you are writing for a certain audience can be inhibiting and this is part of the commonly voiced problem of getting started. My own suggestion is that anyone writing should earmark a file or folder on their hard disc which is entitled 'For my eyes only'. This is for your own thinking and writing, which only they see, which can be later worked up for a critical friend perhaps, and then a supervisor. Uninhibited writing of this kind can help you to find your own position and contribution in producing your thesis.

A third factor which often makes matters worse is the common idea that there is a 'writing up stage'. Surprisingly, many students still talk of being in the 'writing up phase' and universities sometimes still refer to the writing up year of a doctorate. This attitude needs to dispelled as soon as possible in a doctoral programme. Such a shift in attitude and perception alone would help to develop students' writing and address some of the affective barriers outlined above. My view is that we need to promote and encourage in students the view that writing is part of the thinking process, i.e. that writing should be seen as knowledge developing rather than knowledge telling. This implies that writing should start on day one of the postgraduate journey and is a means to develop thinking and understanding – as opposed to a process which simply transfers thoughts from brain to paper, i.e. a mental state to a physical one. As Torrance and Thomas (1994: 109) put it. 'The process of writing is integral to the research process as a whole.'

How can things be improved?

My main argument in this chapter is that students' writing can and should be developed as part of their doctoral journey. Whose responsibility is it to try to develop students' writing? It should be seen as the responsibility of a number of people and groups: certainly the supervisor(s) in giving formative feedback on writing throughout the programme, and we consider this more fully shortly; secondly, many universites provide sessions and workshops on writing, perhaps run by the faculty or the graduate school, depending on how the institution is structured; also, some of the onus lies firmly with the student to make a conscious effort to improve her or his writing skills and develop positive attitudes towards it; and finally, the language teaching centre, or similar set-up, can play an important role.

Probably the central activity in improving students' writing is by providing encouragement, feedback and constructive critique. This is where the supervision process is vital ...

What should students expect of their supervisor?

Earlier in the book we considered in general the issue of what students should expect of supervisors and vice versa. Here we look specifically at writing and the writing process.

First of all, what should students expect of their supervisor(s) when it comes to the business of developing their writing and eventually producing the end product: the dissertation? My list would include the following:

- Praise and encouragement – but honesty too.
- Reading drafts and commenting on them. In the early stages, feedback should be encouraging and supportive. More critical feedback may be needed as the dissertation is developing in its later stages.
- A reasonable expectation of a time lag – acceptable to both sides – between sending in a draft and receiving feedback. Nobody should expect a reply overnight; on the other hand, waiting for three months for feedback is not acceptable in a doctorate which may only last for three or four years. With some pieces of writing (not all), students needs feedback before they can proceed to the next stage and it is essential that this is given in good time.
- Help with overcoming writer's block, whenever it may occur.

- Looking closely at structure and coherence, e.g. use of headings and subheadings.
- Looking at style, grammar and sentence construction, e.g. does every sentence make sense?
- Looking for flow, fluency and linkage as the dissertation nears completion.
- Checking that the student has not 'over-claimed' as a result of their study, e.g. as in 'This thesis makes a paradigm shifting/earth shattering/highly original contribution to the field of X.'

On the other hand, what should supervisors expect of students during the supervisory process, where writing is concerned? My list would include the following:

- that they should at least heed the advice and feedback offered, even if they do not take it all on board – they should engage and interact with it, perhaps during a supervisory meeting or by e-mail;
- that students should ask for specific feedback at times on aspects of their writing, e.g. structure, sentence construction;
- that a suitable, realistic time frame on both sides should be agreed for 'turning writing around', i.e. offering feedback (the supervisor) and responding to it (the student).

From the supervisor's perspective

What are some of the barriers and obstacles to writing that supervisors have seen students face?

Sometimes there are personal issues and insecurities. At other times it's about not being able to stop reading ... or striving for perfectionism. Sometimes students are not prepared to submit even though it's ready.

What strategies do supervisors use to help students with their writing? One supervisor suggests that this is perhaps the most difficult part of the supervision process:

The hardest bit is knowing how to help somebody write, because quite a few students will talk very well and they understand the field and so on ... but they can't write. So I have different strategies for different students. Some I know I have to give small writing tasks to, to improve; others, I know I can say 'do me a seven thousand word chapter' and it's fine. The other thing is, they find it difficult to remember they've got to tell a story – and ultimately the thesis needs to be a straightforward 'telling of a story'. And they tend to want to complicate it too much.

How have other supervisors helped?

> We all have 'writer's block' – and we need to share this. I say: 'If I write 250 words in a day that I'm happy with, and then I've had a good day.' Talking to people and sharing our experiences of writing is so important.

> The first piece of substantive writing can make them genuinely anxious about committing themselves to paper. I try to make each supervision lead to a writing task for them, otherwise it becomes a huge barrier.

> I get them to write from day one and build it up so that 'writing up' is not a barrier.

A recognition of cultural differences

Both parties in the supervision process need to 'bring out into the open' and discuss possible differences in approach to writing the thesis that may result from students' past experiences or varying cultural attitudes to writing. A student may well have implicit, hidden assumptions about how a thesis should be structured, presented and constructed. If these assumptions are kept hidden and they differ from the supervisor's, there may well be a clash. For example, it is said that in Japanese, Chinese, Thai and Korean, the writer often delays the introduction of the purpose of their writing. Such writing might be seen as 'directionless' by a western reader or examiner. One Australian student told me that when writing his master's thesis in Japan, his supervisors expected it to read rather like a detective story, gradually unfolding as it went along. In contrast, students in most western universites are expected to declare the purpose of their work at the start (often including their research questions). The western ideal is to present the thesis in a linear way, showing a sense of development and progression. This may well disguise the fact that the research itself was far from linear, being more 'messy and cyclical' as we discussed earlier, but the convention and the expectation of most examiners, is to present the 'story' using a linear organisation. Similarly, the writer in the western context is expected to:

- provide signposting during the thesis, showing where the writing is going and helping the reader with direction;
- include linkage: joining one idea to another, linking chapters together and generally providing coherence and transition between sections of the thesis;
- make things explicit, i.e. spell things out, such as the contribution which has been made. Leaving things implicit or buried in the text is not part of the convention (as it is in some cultures where this is left to the reader).

All these important conventions and differences need to be discussed during the supervision process to avoid misunderstandings and possible problems at the assessment stage (see Chapter 8 on choosing your examiners).

Finally, another cultural difference which supervisors need to discuss relates to criticality. According to most university regulations for assessing a thesis, students need to take a critical approach to the literature in terms of commenting on it, analysing it and evaluating it. Sillitoe and Crosling (1999: 169) point out that some cultural backgrounds make it difficult for a student to be critical in this western way. For example, a criticism of a text may also be seen as a direct criticism of the author; there may be a cultural respect for the sanctity of the text; there may be greater sensitivity in commenting on others' work or feelings of being impolite.

In view of all the above points, part of the supervision process involves a detailed discussion with students of what it means to be critical, making fully clear the required conventions for the structure and style of thesis presentation in their university.

Guidance on writing

Getting started: when to stop reading and start writing

For most students, and experienced writers, starting a piece of writing is the hardest thing to do, except perhaps for finishing it (or at least knowing when to stop). Getting started on a piece of writing usually involves a kind of build-up to it: various authors have called this cranking up, psyching up, mulling, organising and so on (see Wolcott, 1990: 13, and Woods, 1999). One of the ways of building up is to read widely (making notes on it, distilling thoughts and jotting down your own ideas and viewpoints). The problem of course lies in knowing when to stop reading and to start writing. Initial reading is needed to help in the build-up process (cranking and psyching up) but one has to start writing before finishing reading – mainly because, in a sense, the reading can never stop. Reading should always be done in parallel with writing ('in tandem' as Wolcott, 1990: 21, puts it). The two activities need to be balanced, with reading being on the heavier side of the see-saw initially and writing gradually taking over. Wolcott's view is that writing is a form of thinking and therefore 'you cannot begin writing early enough'.

There is a problematic connection between *reading* and *writing:*

> The move from doing your reading to doing your writing can be a difficult one. I sometimes start by doing just a piece of 'stream of consciousness' writing, to say 'what do I feel about the issues?' Just to break that *fear* of going from 'all these people have written all these things', where do I start? Reading can be inhibiting, it can take away your confidence to write. Reading different things can toss you around like a cork.

Reading is a good way of filling in time and not starting to write. When should we stop? 'When things start to repeat themselves. Reading gives you a feel for what the 'hooks' are, and at least gives you some key headings for what you're writing. Sometimes I read until I find the hook really.

(Both quotations taken from Wellington, 2003)

Ideally, you – the writer – reach a point where your own writing is just waiting to get out there, onto the page. A kind of saturation point is reached. It starts to ooze out. This is the time when we should spend more time writing than we do reading – the balance shifts to the other side. At that stage, ideally, one is impatient to get back to writing. But even then, most of us engage in all sorts of displacement activities: hoovering the hall carpet or walking the dog. Tidying up the hard disk on the computer or checking the e-mails as they come in can also be excellent distractions.

Managing time – or creating it

Dorothea Brande (1983) in her classic book first published in 1934 suggests that a beginning writer should start off by writing for a set period at the same time every day. Once this discipline becomes a habit she suggests that you can write at a different time each day, provided you always set yourself an exact time and keep to it. For many students this advice may be too rigid and impossible to adhere to if one has a busy and unpredictable working day or a complicated home life (as most people now have, even if they did not in 1934). Brande tends to use a physical education (PE) analogy for writing, talking of exercise, training oneself to write, using unused muscles and the value of early morning writing. The PE analogy can be useful to a point (it can be helpful to think of keeping in trim, exercising our writing muscles and taking regular practice) but perhaps should not be overstretched.

One of the great dangers preventing us from finding or creating time to write is the tendency to wait for a big chunk of time to come along when we can 'really get down to it'. People convince themselves that productive writing will happen when they have a large block of uninterrupted time. This is one of the most common forms of procrastination: 'I'll just wait for that day, that weekend, that holiday or that period of study leave and then I can really get some writing done.' Boice (1997: 21) calls this the 'elusive search for large blocks of time. First colleagues wait for intersession breaks. Then sabbaticals. Then retirements.'

Haynes (2001: 12) suggests adopting simple routines for the beginning and end of each session. For example, one could begin with a 'free writing' session of four or five minutes, just bashing out some words and sentences without pausing for correction, revision and certainly not editing. Haynes recounts that he likes to start a new writing session by making revisions to the text that he produced in the last one – a kind of warming up exercise. He also suggests the ploy of finishing a writing session before you have written everything you want to write, with the aim of making you look forward to the next session. Some writers, he claims, even end a session in the middle of a paragraph or even a sentence.

Abby Day (1996: 114–15) suggests that one should limit any writing session to a maximum of two hours. After that, one should take a break, perhaps have a walk or a coffee and come back to it another time feeling refreshed. This is also good health advice if working in front of a screen – most safety guidance suggests short breaks at frequent intervals away from the screen, standing up and looking at distant objects to rest the eyes and neck.

Different ploys, different times of day, different starting strategies will work for different people. The main general advice is to carve out some time to write when it suits your working and domestic day best, and your own preference for your 'best time', and then try to write little and often, not hope for an entire day when you can work uninterrupted. This may never come and, anyway, who can write productively for an entire day? Two or three hours, if you can find them, can yield as much good writing as a solid day that you look forward to with great expectations and then you force yourself to write. However, everyone differs and if you are really one of those people who can't write unless you have a substantial time in which to do it, you will have to find ways of 'clearing the decks' and making it possible.

Working successfully with your supervisor

Attempting to emulate the distinguishing features of skilled, productive writers

Some of the published research into what makes productive writers has provided useful indications of how and when student and supervisor can best work together in improving writing and producing a completed dissertation. For example, Hartley (1997) produced a useful summary of what makes a productive writer in the discipline of psychology. His view was that productive writers exhibit certain strategies. These include:

- completing sections one at a time (however, they don't always do them in order);
- finding quiet conditions in which to write and if possible write in the same place or places;
- setting goals and targets for themselves to achieve;
- write frequently, doing small sections at a time, rather than in long 'binge sessions';
- getting colleagues and friends (including the supervisor) to comment on their early drafts.

These writing strategies should all be considered in trying to make the very most of the supervision process.

Haynes (2001: 11) offers an even shorter list of the qualities of productive writers. From his experience as a commissioning editor, the productive writer:

- seeks advice;
- shares drafts;
- writes regularly (little and often).

Again, these are all ploys which will make the supervision process a more beneficial one.

Getting it off your desk and gradually exposing your writing

Reading your own work is important but is no substitute for having another eye on it, first perhaps from a critical friend, then your supervisor. Later, if possible, you and your supervisor should seek feedback from an 'outsider' – a completely fresh pair of eyes. This is why the upgrade process in many research degrees can be so valuable – the student, and the supervisor, are exposing the work to one or often two completely new people who will read the upgrade paper and ask awkward questions at the upgrade viva (where these procedures are in place in your department).

It is worth leaving your writing to stand for a few weeks before rereading it yourself, but then the supervisor's view and outside reader's if possible are essential too. Richardson (1998) talks of the value of getting early feedback on your writing. This can be achieved by giving an in-progress paper to fellow students in a departmental seminar or using some other public forum such as a conference. In Chapter 9 we give more specific guidance on things that you might ask your friendly reader (or listener) to focus on and provide feedback upon.

Editing, drafting and redrafting

Most writers on writing seem to agree on one thing: do not try to edit and write at the same time (Becker, 1986). Haynes (2001: 111) identifies two parts to the writing process: the compositional and the secretarial. In the first stage, you should concentrate on getting words onto paper, generating text, trying to get the subject matter clear in your own mind and covering the ground. The secretarial stage involves sorting out the structure and layout, correcting things like spelling and punctuation and tinkering around with words and sentences. Haynes describes the first stage as 'writing for the writer', the second as 'writing for the reader'. This second stage is perhaps where the writer really needs to be aware of the intended audience; in the first stage, the writer can care far less about what anyone will think about it, and this slightly carefree attitude can encourage freer writing.

The act of editing can interfere with the activity of writing. Smedley (1993: 29) observes that 'when people first sit down to write, they begin a sentence and immediately take a dislike to the way it is worded and start again. This is the editor interfering with the writer. Both are essential, but both should be kept in their places. 'The writer writes, the editor edits.' She suggests leaving the first draft for a day or a week and coming back to it with your editor's hat on this time. Editing involves seeing if it makes sense, feeling for how well it reads, asking if things could be put more neatly and succinctly and cutting unnecessary words. She argues for a number of drafts: 'Write without editing, then edit, then rewrite without editing, then edit once again. When you exhaust your own critical eye as an editor, enlist the assistance of your spouse, your colleagues, your students, your trusted friends ... and ask them to be brutal' (Smedley, 1993: 30).

Becker (1986) believes that writers can 'start by writing almost anything, any kind of a rough draft, no matter how crude and confused, and make something good out of it'. This could be called the pottery model of writing – start by getting a nice big dollop of clay onto the working area and then set about moulding and shaping. This model may not work for everyone though. Zinsser (1983: 97) talks of feeling that he writes rather like a bricklayer. His thoughts, written at the time by someone who had just discovered the value of the word processor, are worth seeing in full:

> My particular hang-up as a writer is that I have to get every paragraph as nearly right as possible before I go on to the next one. I'm like a bricklayer. I build very slowly, not adding a new row until I feel that the foundation is solid enough to hold up the house. I'm the exact opposite of the writer who dashes off his entire first draft, not caring how sloppy it looks or how badly it's written. His only objective at this early stage is to let his creative motor run the full course at full speed; repairs can always be made later. I envy this writer and would like to have his metabolism. But I'm stuck with the one I've got.

Towards the final stages of editing and revising, a piece of advice given by Harry Wolcott (1990) seems very helpful. He tells of how the idea came to him when he was assembling a new wheelbarrow from a kit: 'Make sure all parts are properly in place before tightening'. Before you start tightening your writing, he argues:

> Take a look at how the whole thing is coming together. Do you have everything you need? And do you need everything you have? (p. 48)

His list of necessary parts includes a statement of our own viewpoints and opinions. We may prefer not to or simply not be willing to, but he believes this will be construed as a 'typical academic cop-out' – a failure to answer the question 'so what?'

> We may prefer not to be pressed for our personal reactions and opinions, but we must be prepared to offer them. It is not unreasonable to expect researchers to have something to contribute as a result of their studied detachment and inquiry-oriented perspective.

In completing a doctorate, people should be expected to voice their own views and draw out the 'so what?' implications. They can do this with due modesty and deference to past literature and research, but without overdoing the usual statement of humility and inadequacy. Wolcott (1990: 69) even argues that a study of even a single case should lead to some judgement and opinion. In answer to the sceptic who challenges 'What can we learn from one case?' Wolcott gives the answer 'All we can.'

A summary: potentially useful guidelines on working with your supervisor on writing

There can be no set of handy hints or infallible guidelines which apply to all writers and genres of writing. Perhaps the main messages of this chapter so far are: writing is part of the thinking process; there is no one right way to write; start writing from day one; draft and redraft; seek feedback so that you don't practise your faults; and 'don't get it right, get it written'. In the list below, I have attempted to crystallise 12 guidelines on how to improve your writing and with the help of your supervisor and others.

1 Don't procrastinate by waiting for the 'perfect opportunity' or the 'ideal writing conditions' such as a free day or a period of study leave before you start writing. They may never come.
2 Don't edit as you write, i.e. as you go along. Wait until later. Composing and revising/editing are different activities (like growing and cooking: Elbow, 1981).
3 Treat writing as a form of thinking. Writing does not proceed by having preset thoughts which are then transformed onto paper: thoughts are created and developed by the process of writing. Writing up your work is an excellent, albeit slightly painful, way of thinking through and making sense of what you have done or what you're doing. This is a good reason for not leaving writing until the end; writing should begin in the first phase or start of your doctoral journey, not the last.

4   Working with your supervisor, break a large piece of writing down into manageable chunks or pieces which will gradually fit together. However, an overall plan is still needed to fit all the pieces together. The job of writing link sentences and link paragraphs joining section to section and chapter to chapter is vital for coherence and fluency. Your supervisor should help you with structure and flow.

5   As well as your supervisor, share your writing with a trusted friend – find a reader/colleague whom you can rely upon to be reliable and just, but critical. Look for somebody else, perhaps someone with no expertise in the area, to read your writing and comment on it. They, and you, should ask: is it clear? Is it readable? Is it well-structured? In other words use other people, use books, e.g. style manuals, books on writing. Do your own proofreading, but always ask someone else to cast an external eye.

6   Draft and redraft; write and rewrite – and don't either expect or try to get it right first time. Writing should not be treated as a 'once and for all' activity. Getting the first draft on to paper is just the first stage. Then 'put it in the ice box and let it cool' (Delton, 1985). Avoid perfectionism.

7   Work with your supervisor to remove unnecessary words; make each word work for a living. After the first draft is on paper go back and check for excess baggage, i.e. redundant words and circumlocution.

8   Be honest with your supervisor about your writing and ultimately your reader. Feel free to admit, in writing, that you found it hard to decide on the right way to, for example, organise your material, decide on a structure, get started, write the conclusion, etc. Don't be afraid to say this in the text (Becker, 1986).

9   Edit 'by ear'; make sure it sounds right and feels right. Treat writing as somewhat like talking to someone except that now you are communicating with the written word. Unlike talking, the reader only has what is on paper. Readers, unlike listeners, do not have body language, tone of voice or any knowledge of you, your background or your thoughts. Writers cannot make the assumptions and short cuts that can be made between talkers and listeners. Have your readers in mind, especially in the later stages of drafting. Better still, visualise one *particular* reader. What will they make of this sentence?

10 Readers need guidance, especially to a long thesis but equally with an article. In the early pages, brief the readers on what they are about to receive. Provide a map to help them navigate through it.

11 Above all, get it 'out of the door' (Becker, 1986) for your supervisor and 'critical friend' reader to look at. Don't sit on it for months, polishing it. Get it off your desk, give it to someone to read (especially your supervisor), then work on it again when it comes back.

12 Finally, two of the most common obstacles to writing are: (a) getting started; (b) writing the abstract and introduction. You can avoid the former by not trying to find the 'one right way' first time round (Becker, 1986), and the latter by leaving the introduction and abstract until last.

This chapter has offered some guidance, reassurance and insight into writing and the writing process. The parting messages are:

- The writing process is a complex one and in some senses is a struggle for many people, but supervisors are there to help you with your writing – it is part of their job.
- Working with them and reflecting on our own writing processes is an essential activity.
- It is also enjoyable and helpful to share your writing and these reflections with peers or a critical friend.
- There is a range of styles and approaches to planning and composing – but there is no one right way of writing. It is hard, often emotional, but rewarding work.

And finally ... another fine balance: meeting expectations of, and audiences for, your writing while preserving your own identity and position

When it comes down to it, the main audience for your own thesis writing (apart from yourself) consists of your supervisor, your internal examiner and your external examiner. In a sense, these are the people you are initially writing your thesis for, especially the latter two. Of course, you may well go on to write up your work for different audiences as you disseminate and publicise it and we consider this in Chapter 11. But the immediate goal of your written dissertation is to give a clear, critical account of your work, its rationale, the literature it is based on, its methodology, its main contributions and its implications for either practice, policy or theory (or sometimes two or all three of these).

This is a tall order and therefore expectations are high. Those expectations put pressure on students to write and present their work in certain ways in order to show their 'academicity' – students can thereby feel stressed by the perceived need to write in a 'scholarly' way, to exhibit their criticality and independence, to 'sound academic', to use some of the jargon in their field and to use certain terms and long words which tend not to be seen or read in any other genre of writing. I have read students' assignments and dissertations where this pressure to sound academic has led them into writing sentences which, although grammatically correct, are completely nonsensical. Here is one I made up earlier (it's quite easy to do): 'The epistemological bias alluded to in Jones' postmodern methodology, coupled with its hegemonic ontology, creates a problematic discourse in which the signifier is foregrounded by the signified.' Translate that if you will (see Wellington, 2000: 153, for further discussion).

I am not suggesting for one moment that terms such as epistemology and ontology should be avoided – they are crucial in discussing any claims to knowledge, how it was arrived at and what its status might be. I am suggesting that writers who are trying to display 'the academic virtues' sometimes fall into the trap of putting together meaningless sentences. Unfortunately, most external (and internal) examiners have the knack of spotting these – a kind of c*** detector.

Some writers are also so pressured by the expectations on them to write in an 'academic' fashion that they relegate their own identity and their own style. In a doctoral thesis, especially perhaps in the social sciences and humanities, it is important that the writer's identity can show through (see Lillis, 2001, for a fuller discussion of identity). Ultimately, the author of a dissertation has to have a thesis – translated literally from the Greek as a position. In bringing this thesis out of the dissertation, the student as a writer needs to have some sense of independence and identity – while also following the rules and conventions of academic writing. This is the great challenge in producing a dissertation – balancing the expectations of academia with the requirement to contribute, to have a position and an argument, and to retain one's identity. It is a fine balance, which the supervision process plays a central role in maintaining.

 **Further reading**

Becker, H. (1986) *Writing for Social Scientists*. Chicago: Chicago University Press.

Brause, R. S. (2000) *Writing Your Doctoral Dissertation: Invisible Rules for Success*. London: Falmer.

Murray, R. (2002) *How to Write a Thesis*. Maidenhead: Open University Press.

Rudestam, K. and Newton, R. (1992) *Surviving Your Dissertation*. London: Sage.

Wellingon, J., Bathmaker, A., Hunt, C., McCulloch, G. and Sikes, P. (2005) *Succeeding with Your Doctorate*. London: Sage.

Wolcott, H. (1990) *Writing Up Qualitative Research*. Newbury Park, CA: Sage.

Woods, P. (1999) *Successful Writing for Qualitative Researchers*. London: Routledge.

Choosing your examiners

Chapter aims

It hardly needs to be said that the business of choosing your examiners is a vitally important part of the doctoral journey. The examiners will be the two people who will read your thesis most closely with a fresh pair of eyes. They will be the people deciding upon and asking the questions at the viva; they are the people who will interact together and decide how the viva will be conducted; and they are the people making the key decisions about your work after the viva has finished. As well as judging your work, they are also the two people who should give you the best *formative* feedback as a result of the viva, if it is conducted properly (see Chapter 10 on the viva).

In short, the choice of examiners is a major decision to which all those involved need to give lengthy thought and consideration. Hence a chapter, albeit a short one, is devoted to this choice.

Who should be involved in the decision?

Normally, the supervisor has the main responsibility for identifying an internal and external examiner. After that, the department, usually through the head of research degrees (often called the postgraduate tutor), check the suggested combination of examiners and if approved will take matters to the next stage, i.e. having arrived at a short list of two (internal and external) they are approached to see if they are willing and able to read the thesis and conduct the viva in the right time frame (regulations require a time limit of about ten weeks between submitting your thesis and holding the viva). Often, the research degrees secretary fills in the necessary form which then has to be approved at faculty level and the process can begin. In some universities, an independent chair is also involved in making the arrangements and will also be present at the viva itself.

However, although matters are expedited by staff, the department will often (and in my view should) welcome students' involvement in suggesting both examiners, even though the final decision will be made by staff. Incidentally, in many cases, it is the responsibility of the internal examiner to actually arrange the viva, ensuring the external examiner receives a copy of the thesis well in advance of the viva and making sure that all the necessary arrangements are put in place (further details about the internal/examiner role will be provided by the university you are working in).

Many departments will have long experience in choosing appropriate examiners – they will draw on this and on their knowledge of how examiners have 'behaved' in the past, as well as their own experiences of meeting and working with people around the world. However, this does not mean that students cannot or should not play an active part in making this important decision. This chapter provides a student's perspective on how that might be done and which criteria might be brought to bear.

When should you start considering the choice?

In a way, the answer to this is the sooner the better, provided that it does not create anxiety at an early stage, e.g. by having the thought of the likely audience for your writing in mind at all times – as we have seen, this can be an inhibiting factor when writing. Equally, the doctoral journey never did run smooth and the two people one might want as examiners in the first year may be completely dismissed as possibilities when year three arrives.

When should they actually be arranged?

It is always good practice to produce a draft dissertation which can then be looked at critically as a whole. This draft will be close to the finished product but is likely to be in a temporary binding. Incidentally, being able to see, and physically hold, this almost completed work is likely to be a great boost to many students who have toiled for a number of years to reach this stage. At this point, the final draft can be given to at least one critical reader (in addition to the supervisor) to view it in its entirety with the first fresh pair of eyes. Many departments have a policy that the draft should be read by one, or in some cases two, academic colleagues who have had nothing to do with the supervision process. In other cases, the student him or herself can arrange for a critical friend to evaluate the near-finished product. This critical reading can be of great benefit in moving to the final phase and in preparing for the viva. These fresh readers may also have valuable suggestions for possible internal and external examiners.

After that point, it is good practice to start to firm up the choice of examiners. They will need to be contacted (though not by the student!) with rough dates in mind for a viva. If they happen to be unavailable for a long period then the choice may have to begin again. It is always best to give one's carefully chosen potential examiners at least a few months notice in order to increase the chance of their being willing and available.

Pinning down names

The best choice of examiner may not necessarily be the person who is perceived as the expert in your field. Nor should it necessarily be the person whose work you have referenced the most in writing your dissertation. There are other, more important, criteria that should determine who and **who not to** choose.

For example, clearly neither student nor supervisor will want external examiners who might be pompous, have inflated opinions of themselves, who talk too much, who could be awkward or aggressive, or who could arrive on the day of the viva with too many 'bees in their bonnet' (don't worry, these are few and far between). Experienced staff in your department (for example, the head of research degrees) should know who these people are and how to avoid them.

On a more positive note, several questions should be borne in mind when suggesting examiners:

- Will they be sympathetic towards the aims of your research? Will they be familiar with and sympathetic to your field of study and methodology?
- Do you and your supervisor know their work and their personal qualities?
- Have you met either internal or external examiner before? (Do not worry if not.) Would you feel comfortable with them in a viva situation?
- Has the external examiner examined in your department before? (If not, this may well be a good opportunity to involve someone new.)
- For professional doctorate (PD) students, has at least one of them examined a PD before?
- Is the external examiner likely to be fair, thorough and challenging, without being aggressive or overbearing?

- Will they come to the viva with any sort of agenda?
- The combination or chemistry between internal and external examiners is important: will they work well together in planning the viva, asking questions and deciding jointly on a recommendation after the oral? (This is difficult to assess, but worth considering.)

We look at each of these in turn.

Will the examiners be sympathetic towards the aims of your research?

This is probably the first question to consider. For example, if in the social sciences you are writing from (say) a feminist or Marxist or neo-liberal perspective it might not be a good idea to choose someone with totally opposing ideologies. Similarly with methodology: if you have adopted a quantitative approach to research design, sampling and data collection then examiners who are firmly in the qualitative paradigm may not be a good choice. Even within such paradigms it pays to consider carefully which specific approach examiners are most likely to connect with, for example grounded theory, ethnography, auto-ethnography, action research and so on. You are not looking for perfect compatibility or congruence with your aims and methodology – but you should certainly be looking for empathy with it.

Do you and your supervisor know their work?

For the reasons above, it is important to know as much as possible about the reputation and publications of the external examiner especially, but also those of the internal examiners. Which field has most of their work been in? Are they currently working and writing in this area? What methodological approach have they taken in their past research? Are they likely to be empathetic towards your aims, approach and methods?

Have you met either internal or external examiner before? Would you feel comfortable with them in a viva situation?

We discussed in an earlier chapter the observation that producing a doctorate concerns a lot more than just cognition, i.e. skills, knowledge and understanding. It involves the affective domain, i.e. feelings, attitudes and emotions, in almost equal measure. This also applies to the choice of examiner – as well as to the viva itself (as we discuss in Chapter 10). Hence the decision involves, to put it bluntly, personal considerations. If you have met and interacted with the examiners before then your feelings about that interaction are highly relevant. You may have heard, seen or chatted to a potential external examiner at a conference or a meeting. That can be very useful and the fact that you have discussed your work or theirs with them does not rule that person out (if they had become a close friend or regular correspondent then the situation would be more cloudy). Equally, previous meetings or interactions with your potential internal examiner will not exclude that person, provided that he or she has not already given you detailed feedback on your work.

However, it may be the case that you have not met either your external or your internal examiner before (though the latter is unlikely in most departments). This need not be a problem, provided you and your supervisor have done some research into their work and their personal reputation, as far as that is possible.

Has the external examiner examined in your department before?

Firstly, if not, then this may well be a good opportunity to involve or induct someone new into the work of the department and to add to its list of potential examiners. However, the provisos already discussed must come into the decision. All of the following questions need to be addressed: do you know how they behave as an external? Have they examined elsewhere before and how did it go? Is their methodological approach appropriate? Is there likely to be any clash of ideologies?

It is worth emphasising again that the perceived national expert in your field, or the person you make most reference to in your bibliography, may not always make the ideal external examiner. Academic credentials and criteria are important but they are not the only vital ones in this crucial decision.

Probably the key question to ask should be: is the external examiner likely to be fair, thorough and challenging, without being aggressive or overbearing?

For professional doctorate (PD) students, has at least one of the examiners examined a PD before?

Although the criteria stated in most university regulations are broadly similar for a PD thesis and for a traditional PhD, they are always open to interpretation by examiners. Terms such as originality, publishability and contribution have a wide range of meanings and connotations. In the context of a PD, which is often designed to relate to and impact upon the student's professional practice, the tone and modus operandi of the oral examination may be very different to that of a PhD, even if all the written regulations are the same. Examiners bring with them their own preconceptions ('baggage' to use the slang) depending on their own background, their own doctorate and in some cases their own prejudices towards a 'professional' doctorate.

I have even experienced a viva where an external examiner has said of the PD student's thesis something along the lines of 'this is a very good study – with a little more work you could make it into a PhD.' I have also met examiners who have feigned a kind of naive ignorance about the professional doctorate, constantly asking how it compares to the PhD and how it differs from it.

My own view is that examiners for a PD should be selected who view the current diversity of doctorates positively, who have experience of the PD themselves and who are prepared to be open minded about the purposes and the quality of professional doctorates, while being rigorous and thorough in the assessment of them.

Will they come to the viva with any sort of agenda?

This question is very similar to the two above but is worth further discussion. Every person carries some sort of agenda in the sense of having prior conceptions and views (without our conceptions how could we possibly make sense of the world, to paraphrase the philosopher Immanuel Kant). These views and preconceptions are inevitably brought to the examination of a written thesis and the subsequent viva. The issue is: to what extent could they or would they prevent a fair, rigorous and thorough assessment of a student's work?

We have discussed some possibilities above, such as ideological, method-ological or philosophical mismatch (incongruence) between examiner and student. But there are other agendas to be wary of, sometimes of a very per-sonal nature. Is there a 'history' between the potential examiner and anyone in your department? This may not be either the supervisor or the student (which would be serious), but it may involve a colleague not connected with that particular supervision process.

Does one of the examiners come to the assessment process with something to prove? Or to use it as an opportunity to show themselves off and blow their own trumpet?

If an external examiner is invited who was formerly in the department (usually acceptable after a gap of at least three years) are they going to use the examination process as a platform to show, for example, how far they have come since leaving the department? Or are they carrying any lingering resentment towards the department that has fermented since leaving?

Is there likely to be any clash of views or philosophy between one of the examiners and the supervisor? On a more sinister note, is there any tension between the proposed internal examiner and the supervisor – I have wit-nessed, or sensed, this myself as an external examiner at other universities.

Will the internal and external examiners work well together in planning the viva, asking questions and deciding jointly on a recommendation after the oral?

The situation would be especially serious if there were some sort of background or latent disagreement between the proposed internal and the external examiners. In my experience this possible tension can and certainly should be avoided if the decision is made carefully.

A healthy combination or chemistry between the two examiners is essential. For a good examination process the two examiners should work well together in at least the following ways:

- They should not disagree fundamentally about basic issues in research approach, design or philosophy.
- They should interact well and be capable of working together in creating a dialogue and making an agreed decision, i.e. a consensus.
- There should not be a huge 'power imbalance' between the internal and external examiners.
- Both should carry equal weight and one should not be bullied or talked into a decision by the other.

And finally ... the people to avoid

There are certain types of academic who are well worth avoiding when it comes to making the final choice. These may be idealised types but it is surprising how often I have witnessed aspects of the following behaviours in a viva. Diana Leonard (2001) suggests the following labels for the people to avoid and I have given my own brief description of each one:

1 The *'proofreader'*. This is the person who checks every comma, full stop and sentence, who delights in spotting typing errors, who spends valuable time during the viva in pointing them out (one by one) and who is generally one of the most pedantic people you have met.
2 The *'committee man'*. This examiner is similar to the proofreader and spends the entire viva going through page by page from start to finish.
3 The *'hobby horse rider'*. This is the person who comes with bees in their bonnet, agendas and will commonly say 'I see you haven't quoted my old pal Bloggs here' – or more annoyingly that you have not quoted them on every page.
4 The *'kite flyer'*. Similarly, the 'kite flyer' has lots of bees in their bonnet and asks questions that are only tenuously related to your thesis – they wonder why you did not write the thesis they would have wanted rather than the one you did write.

5   *The 'reminiscer'.* This is the (probably 'mature') examiner who uses the viva as an opportunity to look back on old times, to tell stories and anecdotes, to name drop and generally reminisce on the halcyon days of academia.

(Diana Leonard's discussion is based
on Brown and Atkins, 1988)

In conclusion ...

There are a number of criteria to be borne in mind and questions to pose when making the important decision around who to invite to examine your work. One should never assume that the renowned expert in the field, whose work has been cited prolifically in your references, is the obvious choice. This chapter is premised on the view that students can and should play an active role in considering examiners for their work, even though the final decision and the subsequent process must be led by the department. Many of the questions that might be posed in deliberating on the choice of examiners have been considered.

I hope that this chapter has not given the impression that the academic world is teeming with possible examiners who may be unfair, pompous and carrying unwanted bees in their bonnets. Nothing could be further from the truth in my own experience – the norm is for examiners to be fair, thorough, rigorous, respectful and civil. This is often realised in the conduct of the viva, which we look at in detail in Chapter 10.

In the next chapter we discuss the business of preparing your dissertation for submission and how this relates to your choice of examiners. We finish this chapter with a pertinent quote from one of the supervisors I interviewed:

My own confidence has grown as I have supervised more and more, so that I can encourage my students to be more radical in the way they present their thesis. Also, the culture for what is acceptable has widened. However, not playing it safe brings two requirements: it needs to be higher quality; and we need to choose examiners for it very carefully.

 Further reading

Joyner, R. (2003) 'The selection of external examiners for research degrees', *Quality in Higher Education*, 11 (2): 123–7.
Mullins, G. and Kiley, M. (2002) 'It's a PhD, not a Nobel Prize: how experienced examiners assess research theses', *Studies in Higher Education*, 27 (4): 369–86.

9

Submitting your dissertation and preparing for assessment

 Chapter aims

This chapter considers:

- the interaction between the written and oral aspects of assessment;
- what needs to be done before final submission;
- the traditional structure for a dissertation;
- regulations from different universities;
- what the key criteria are and what they mean to people;
- different interpretations of what makes a 'good' thesis;
- what examiners actually look for.

Introduction

In this chapter we focus on the written thesis. Chapter 10 looks at the oral examination.

In previous chapters we have looked at the business of 'getting the thesis written' and how to work with your supervisor in achieving this major (probably *the* major) goal. We also looked at the best time and the best way of choosing examiners for the written thesis and the viva voce. In Chapter 8, it was suggested that the best time for 'firming up' the choice is at or around the time when the final draft of the dissertation is complete and these draft chapters have been put together in some tangible form, perhaps a temporary binding, which looks like the 'embodiment of a thesis'!

The next stage is to prepare for the examination process, i.e. the critical reading of your thesis by two carefully selected examiners and the subsequent oral examination. Both form separate parts of the assessment stage, so this book devotes a chapter to each. However, as the next two chapters show, the two facets of the examination are closely related: for example, the examiners' reading of the written thesis (which is done before the viva) will play a major part in shaping their conduct, their attitude and approach to and to some extent their views on the purpose of the viva.

Equally, the viva itself (which is an essential and influential part of the assessment process) may shape the examiners' attitudes to and judgement on the written thesis. For example, a good viva can help to clarify, to bring to life and to justify the work and ideas presented in written form. In short, the two parts of the assessment should be seen in tandem because they exert a mutual influence on each other.

Before final submission ...

You will have worked for a number of years one hopes in a productive and close relationship with your supervisor towards the goal of having a finished 'product' in the required written format ready to submit for assessment. This is at once the great value but also the inherent drawback of the supervision process. Both sides of the relationship, even where there has been successful co-supervision, have become very close to the finished product. For this reason, it is essential that some third party, who has never set eyes on the thesis before, is asked to take a critical look at the written thesis before it is finally bound and dispatched.

Some departments have a policy that this must be done before the work can be submitted. I even know of one department which insists on two people looking over the final draft before binding and submission. Clearly, this makes extra work for people in that department and this may be problematic in a small department. It also means that the 'critical reader' at this stage is prevented from being the internal examiner, so careful choices and decisions have to be made.

Whatever procedure or policy is adopted the main action point is that someone totally 'fresh' to the work should be asked to read it. Reading your own work is important but is no substitute for having another eye on it. It is essential that your supervisor(s) should read the draft first; I have come across horror stories (with unhappy endings) where the student has gone ahead and formally submitted without the supervisor having seen the final version. But once your supervisor has approved the final draft, it really should go to a new, critical reader before the final, formal submission stage. Ideally, this should be another member of staff in the department but I have come across cases of critical readers being a student's colleague, a former peer who has recently completed or even a peer at a similar stage.

What should your reader be asked to look for?

We have discussed in previous chapters of this book the importance of asking for feedback on one's writing and, within this general point, the value of asking readers to look for specific things. What should you ask people to look for at this stage?

1 *Ellipsis.* The writer's own tacit, implicit knowledge of what they wish to say makes it hard to identify the missing elements or steps in their own writing that are somewhere in their head but have not made it out onto the paper. These may be missing episodes in an account or missing steps in an argument, so that the writer seems to jump to a conclusion without adequate premises. The Greek word 'ellipsis' (meaning 'cutting short') seems to sum up these omissions neatly. Readers can spot a writer's ellipses more readily than writers can spot their own.

2 *Sentences, flow and sound.* Similarly, readers can also identify sentences that are clumsy, too long or simply don't read well or sound right. It is also easier to spot long-windedness or repetition in someone else's writing than in your own. Wolcott (1990: 46) suggests that reading your own words aloud to yourself can help, but even better a friend or colleague (it would need to be a good one) could read them to you so that you can listen to and concentrate on 'what has actually reached paper – the experience you are creating for others, out of your own experience.' When the oral reader stumbles or 'gasps for air' (as Wolcott puts it) then it is time to 'get busy with the editing pencil'.

3 *Structure and coherence (a 'pathway').* The new reader can be asked to judge whether the structure and pathway through the thesis are clear and coherent. Does the written dissertation tell the story of what was done in a clear way? This can be followed up in the viva of course, but it is best to make this transparent in written form. Does the dissertation hang together well? Are there clear links between the chapters, e.g. the literature review and the methodology, the findings and the previous literature in the area?

4 *Is there a clear thesis?* The Greek word 'thesis' literally means 'position'. Every dissertation should present a thesis in the sense of having a position or an argument. Is this made clear and explicit? Is the contribution made by the study brought out and emphasised for the reader?

More laboriously, if you can find a fresh reader to check right through your dissertation for 'typos' then that person will be worth his or her weight in gold. A spellchecker alone is not adequate. From my experience of examining, it is very rare for a dissertation to be free of typos. However, an excessive number will indicate to the examiner that it has not been proofread and more generally indicates a lack of care and attention to detail which will raise the hackles of many an examiner. Some may even see the presence of excessive typographical errors, especially if coupled with poor presentation, as being disrespectful.

Perhaps the ultimate question that every student needs to consider and discuss in detail with their supervisor(s) is quite simply: is it *ready* to be submitted? This is not a decision that students can make or should make on their own. From the supervisor's view too, it is always helpful to have a third or fourth opinion. This is where the release of the final draft to a new reader plays such an important part. People with experience of supervising and examining research degrees can usually gauge when a thesis is ready for submission, even if they cannot state explicitly the criteria by which they make that judgement. In the next few sections we consider and discuss what those criteria might be.

The final submission

Different universities have different regulations and guidelines on submission and this needs to be thoroughly checked and adhered to. It is always best to play strictly by the rules, not least those concerning technical issues. These are likely to include: size of typeface and margins, line spacing, formatting of quotations, total word length, styles of referencing, use of headings and subheadings, appendices and all the other important issues concerning presentation. The surest way to displease examiners is to present the dissertation poorly, to include typographical errors and to ignore guidelines on technical matters. In short, presentation of a high quality is a necessary (though not sufficient) condition of success. Incidentally, this is certainly something that your fresh pair of eyes should be asked to give their view on.

Beyond issues of presentation, few university guidelines, in my experience as an external examiner, provide a detailed prescription of what a written dissertation should contain let alone what might be included in individual chapters. One valuable exception is provided by the guidelines I received from the University of Newcastle in 2004 as one of their external examiners for a research degree. The *Handbook for Examiners* gave a comprehensive list of 'Criteria related to chapters of the work' (section 5.1.1). This guidance was prefaced by the statement that specific chapters do vary enormously from one subject and one topic to another but they may well include material on:

- the context of the study (academic but possibly also 'industrial or commercial');
- the literature: these chapter(s) should contain a 'critical review' and should make 'explicit links' with other parts of the thesis;
- the methodology and methods: an 'awareness of the range' which might have been used, a justification of those actually used', 'practical problems and issues' encountered, ethical considerations, where applicable;
- the design of the study, including its limitations;
- analysis, e.g. an account of the empirical techniques used;
- outcomes/results, including a 'justification' of how these outcomes are based on the 'analysis of the evidence', and a summary of 'patterns and trends' in the results;
- discussion of the 'main points' emerging from the results, an awareness of the limitations of the outcomes;
- conclusions: this should include a justification for them and a discussion of the 'implications of the conclusions for the field of knowledge'.

This bullet point list is merely a summary of the section in the Newcastle Handbook, which I found very useful as an external examiner. I feel that it is also a useful guide for students and supervisors in making their own 'self-assessment' of their draft thesis prior to submission. The Handbook also gives more general criteria for the written thesis, including the requirements, which I summarise below, that it should be:

- *authentic* – i.e. the candidate's own work and all sources used should be correctly acknowledged;
- *scholarly* – it should display 'critical discrimination and a sense of proportion in evaluating evidence and the opinions of others';
- *professional* – the candidate should demonstrate that they have 'acquired' a 'repertoire' of research skills appropriate to a researcher in the field of study;
- *well-structured, written and presented* – the dissertation 'should be orderly in arrangement, well-written and presented'.

Incidentally, some of these qualities, especially the first and third bullet points, are likely to be probed in some depth in the viva, as we see in the next chapter.

The traditional structure for a dissertation

There is no fixed or set way in which a dissertation should be structured. Presentation, ordering of contents and chapter headings can vary enormously, depending on all sorts of factors. However, I do find from experience that many written theses do follow some kind of pattern. This is shown in Table 9.1, which often goes as far as being translated into chapter headings along these lines.

Table 9.1   The traditional structure for a dissertation

Abstract	e.g. What you did Why it is important How you did it Key findings
Introduction	e.g. Main aims Key research questions Scene-setting/the context of the study A 'map' for the reader
Literature review	e.g. Main areas covered Why these Why not others Links with other parts of the dissertation Theoretical frameworks used and why these
Methodology and methods	Research design and approach Which methods Why these The sample Gaining access (if an empirical study) Ethical issues
Results/findings/analysis	Analysis approach and technique Theoretical frameworks used
Discussion and evaluation	Reflection on both findings and methods Relation to existing literature
Conclusions and recommendations	Contributions Limitations 'So what ...?' What are the implications of your work? Ideas for further research
Appendices	e.g. Interview schedule Detailed tables of data Ethical procedures
References/bibliography	Full list of all sources cited above

I am not suggesting that the framework shown here should act as a kind of template for a dissertation, although I have known supervisors who do see it almost in that way. There are ways of deviating from this norm and of presenting a dissertation in a totally different format, many of which will be acceptable. These are always interesting and often creative, but I still feel that it is important to have a conventional framework in mind that one can deviate from! Again, these are issues that will need to be discussed with your supervisor(s), bearing in mind who the examiners are likely to be and how they will receive a dissertation which does not follow a traditional framework.

For a much fuller discussion of these important decisions on how to present and structure your thesis, see Wellington et al. (2005). Chapter 9 of that book gives full details on producing a doctoral thesis along traditional lines while Chapter 8 discusses alternative approaches to presenting theses, covering auto-ethnography, ethnographic fiction, poetry, dramatic presentations, mixed genres and other alternative styles. As we say there: 'Getting the support of your supervisor and also enlisting sympathetic examiners is crucial if you are going to adopt what might be termed as "alternative" approaches' (Wellington et al., 2005: 157).

Writing your abstract – quite a challenge

This is worth focusing on for a simple reason: one of the hardest things to write for a thesis (or for an article for that matter) is the abstract. Yet this is one of the most important single pages of the thesis, which in my experience is one of the *first* things to be read by the examiners. For this reason alone, it is well worth spending time on – perhaps drafting and redrafting several times over, having it checked and rechecked until it is as near perfect as you can make it. It is often the last piece of the thesis to be finally written.

Essentially, it is a summary of your thesis. Your abstract should include, in no more than about 300 words under most regulations, a few sentences on:

- your aims/purpose(s);
- what you actually did;
- why you did it and why it is important;
- how you did it;
- with whom, where and when you did it (for empirical studies);
- the key findings;
- 'so what'...?', i.e. what are the implications of what you have done and why does it matter.

This all needs to be achieved, under most regulations, in an overall total of about *10 to 15 sentences* – that is quite a tall order. It should not include references or quotations.

Regulations from different universities

We saw in Chapter 6 that regulations on the requirements of a research degree thesis vary widely and are open to interpretation. Thus one university (Newcastle) states that a key criterion for a postgraduate thesis is that it should show evidence of 'industry and application'. The difficulty here of course is that the level of industry is hard to define and will vary enormously from one topic, discipline or student to another.

Their Handbook also states that a thesis should show that the 'candidate understands the relationship of the theme of his or her thesis to the wider field of knowledge'. They also state that it should show evidence of 'original scholarship' and contain material 'worthy of publication'.

Other regulations, from other universities, use similar terms such as: original work, evidence of systematic study, the ability to conduct original investigations, able to test ideas, understands the relationship of the theme of the thesis to the wider field of knowledge, worthy of publication (on many occasions), makes a distinct contribution to knowledge, forms a coherent and substantial body of work, shows independent critical ability, clearly written, takes due account of previously published work on the subject ... and so on.

As we saw in Chapter 6, many of these terms are problematic. My own interviews with supervisors show the difficulty with the most widely used term in postgraduate regulations: originality. For example:

> Originality? I don't think we know what we mean by it – it stretches across a wide continuum. Some very good PhDs build on an original idea that someone else has had ... some don't. Publishable? Again it means different things – I think what is sad is that many of them (postgraduate students) don't publish.

> Originality comes in all sorts of different ways and shapes; there are different ways of saying things and of seeing things.

Examiners' interpretations of what makes a good thesis

One way of finding out how different examiners actually go about interpreting the stated criteria for theses (assuming, that is, that they read them) is to ask them some key questions: what do they actually look for when reading a thesis? (including the question, what is the first thing they look at or for when the thesis arrives on their desk?) What do they consider makes a 'good thesis'? What are the key factors or criteria *for them*?

Views from informal discussions

Over the last ten years or more I have done this informally with a range of experienced examiners. A range of things has been said to me and I regret that I have not recorded them more systematically. The first interesting thing is that many people whom I have spoken to tell me that the first part of the dissertation they look at it when they first open it is the abstract. This is hardly surprising but it does reinforce the point made earlier that time needs to be devoted to this, it should be drafted and redrafted several times, and (last but not least) this is the part of the dissertation which above all others should not contain any typos! As for informal comments on what people consider to be a good dissertation here is my paraphrase of some of the main points which have been expressed to me:

- It should be clear what the thesis is about and what its contribution is.
- It should not be over-ambitious, either in making exaggerated claims for its contribution or raising the reader's expectations too highly and unrealistically, i.e. it does what it says it is going to do (in modern advertising parlance, one could say 'it does what it says on the tin').
- The data collection is linked to the theoretical discussions and the literature review, i.e. the empirical work is closely linked to the theoretical work and the data are fully used and connected to the rest of the dissertation (the student has not been guilty of 'over-collecting and under-analysing' or not fully discussing her or his data).
- Presentation: the writing is clear, jargon is not over-used and it has a clear structure.

Views on what makes a bad thesis are the converse of the above: the reader does not know what the thesis is about; it is over-ambitious and does not achieve what it set out to do or said in the early sections it would be doing; the theory sections and the literature review are not linked to the empirical work; the data are 'under-used'; the structure and the writing itself are not clear.

What makes a good thesis – my own view

My informal discussions with other colleagues, examiners and supervisors over a long period have shaped my own, personal views. In general, my perception of a good dissertation is that it should have the following characteristics:

- A wide range of relevant literature is critically discussed (including at least one or two references which make the reader say 'Ah! That's a new one').
- It is well structured, signposted and clear to follow; the different parts of the thesis link together and 'knit well' to make a coherent whole.
- The researcher has managed to link his or her work to the work of others.
- Methods and methodology (including ethical issues) are deliberated upon before discussion of the researcher's own empirical work.
- The researcher is honest and open about the methods used, and why, and reflects on methods and methodology after presenting and discussing her or his own work.
- There are no obvious spelling or grammatical errors, typos, clumsy sentences or incorrect use of words (e.g. persistent use of: effect for affect; criterion for criteria; it's for its; or misused apostrophes).

- Some attempt is made to draw out implications, and lessons which can be learned from it are made explicit, i.e. the implications for policy-makers or practitioners, or both, are drawn out.
- Limitations of the study are discussed (without being too apologetic) and areas for further research are suggested.
- The dissertation **contributes** to the 'public store of knowledge' (even, perhaps, the 'public good') and not just to the writer's own personal development.

Perhaps above all, for me as a reader or examiner, the written thesis (and every sentence in it) should 'make sense'!

Criteria for assessing the written thesis

Someone who has looked at criteria more systematically than I have is Professor Pam Denicolo, Director of the Social Sciences Graduate School at the University of Reading, who has long experience of supervising and examining PhD theses. She began reflecting on assessment criteria by putting her own tacit, implicit criteria on paper; she then distributed her list to a range of experienced colleagues, who added to it and amended it.

Pam has given permission to reproduce the resulting summary of 'attributes that examiners would look for in a thesis' below. She points out that the specific detail and the balance between criteria will vary from one topic area and discipline to another.

Overall

- Careful, clear presentation that has the reader's needs in mind.
- If necessary, or helpful, a glossary of terms and/or of acronyms preceding the main text and succeeding the contents list.
- The contribution to knowledge expected and achieved should be made explicit.
- Each chapter should be coherent in itself and contribute to an integrated whole.
- Fulfils the institutional requirements for presentation (margins, spacing, font size and character).

Sectional attributes

- **Abstract**
  - Clearly describes main aspects of the thesis within the word limit.

- **Introduction**
  - Rationale for study clearly explicated.
  - The appropriateness of this researcher conducting this study made clear.
  - Brief overview of thesis provided, demonstrating the 'story line' chapter by chapter.

- *Review of relevant literature*
  - Succinct, penetrating, challenging, critical, analytical approach.
  - Demonstration of thorough knowledge of field.
  - Primary rather than secondary sources used.
  - Recent references except for seminal work acknowledged.
  - Quotations (NB page numbers required) used to illustrate or exemplify rather than substitute for own words in argument.

- *Statement of research problems*
  - Clear and succinct hypotheses or questions derived from/revealed by the literature review.
  - Should have a novel theoretical or methodological slant and/or bring together previously unrelated fields and/or a new area of application.
  - Well articulated rationale for 'worthwhileness' of research.

- *Approach and methods of enquiry adopted (theoretical argument-methodology rather than 'methods')*
  - Rationale of general approach closely argued giving reasoned case for rejecting other possible approaches.
  - Justification of research design presented, taking account of potential advantages and limitations.
  - Research techniques argued as theoretically and practically relevant to research problem; reasons given for rejection of possible alternatives; rationale provided for amendments to standard tests and procedures or for detailed design of innovative techniques.
  - Rationale provided for the selection of the analysis procedures, choice of statistical tests, etc.

- *Fieldwork/labwork (description of actual process)*
  - Clearly set out and easy to follow.
  - Relevant details included (how access was achieved, number of subjects/ respondents, relevant profiles, timing of interventions, duration of inter- ventions, etc. or what materials and equipment were used, what proce- dures were followed, etc.).
  - Ethical issues – what permissions were obtained, what guarantees were given, how ethical issues have been acknowledged and dealt with.
  - Difficulties encountered and how they were dealt with so that the research was not compromised.

- *Analysis of data*
  - Mode of analysis theoretically justified.
  - Any assumptions stated and justified.
  - Congruent with research questions/hypotheses and approach adopted.
  - Details of procedure clearly presented.

- *Presentation of data*
  - Clearly structured.
  - Data 'trail' evident.
  - Details of why, who, what, when and where provided.
  - Tables, figures, diagrams to summarise data clearly numbered and titled and referred to in the text.

- *Discussion of outcomes*
  - Main points summarised and evaluated; interpretations made of raw data.
  - Links made to literature previously presented, e.g. what previous research/theory has been supported, substantiated, challenged, amended, rejected, etc.
  - Reflections on the research process – limitations addressed and consequent implications for results.
  - Suggestions for repeat or further research based on this research.
  - Implications of results for theory and for practice.
  - Clear articulation of contribution to knowledge.

- *References*
  - All references in the text included in an appropriate style.
  - No references included that do not appear in the text – but a separate, short bibliography of influential texts is acceptable.

- *Appendices*
  - all appendices clearly numbered in the order of appearance in the main text.

(The above list is reproduced with the kind permission of Professor Pam Denicolo, University of Reading.)

I find the above list of criteria or attributes provided by Professor Denicolo to be extremely useful, not least in helping students to reflect on the final draft of their dissertation and to aid their preparation for the viva voce.

In conclusion ...

This chapter has focused on the vital activity of preparing your written thesis for submission. The chapter has considered the importance of 'exposing' your final draft to a fresh reader (or two) prior to the final submission. We have considered what a reader at this stage should be looking for in order to help in the difficult judgement of whether the 'thesis is ready'. Many universities give guidance on the final submission, and attending to this is a vital part of the supervision process. There seems to be some common understanding of how a thesis might be structured although there is no reason why supervisor and student should not discuss alternative ways of presenting and structuring written work. Finally, the chapter has reflected on the range of criteria for judging the written thesis that are stated in regulations – but these are open to interpretation by the human beings who are chosen to be the examiners of the written text. Different interpretations and viewpoints on 'what makes a good thesis' have been presented. These are offered for reflection and discussion. They can be used in the supervision process as an important element in the business of deciding whether a thesis is ready for submission or not.

The examiners' reading of the written thesis is the first part of the assessment process. It will shape and influence the second part of the process – the oral examination – which we focus on in the next chapter.

 Further reading

Brause, R. S. (2000) *Writing Your Doctoral Dissertation: Invisible Rules for Success.* London: Falmer.

Murray, R. (2002) *How to Write a Thesis.* Maidenhead: Open University Press.

Parry, S. (2007) *Disciplines and Doctorates.* Dordrecht: Springer. Discusses in depth the implicit 'protocols and parameters' that govern the award of the doctorate in different disciplines, based on her study across a range of Australian universities.

Pearce, L. (2005) *How to Examine a Thesis.* Buckingham: SRHE/Open University Press. Written from an examiner's perspective includes sections on criteria, regulations, procedures and the roles of examiners.

Rudestam, K. and Newton, R. (1992) *Surviving Your Dissertation.* London: Sage.

Wellington, J., Bathmaker, A. M., Hunt, C., McCulloch, G. and Sikes, P. (2005) *Succeeding with Your Doctorate.* London: Sage, chapters 8 and 9.

10

Preparing for the live event - the viva voce

Chapter aims

This chapter considers:

- students' feelings, anticipations and expectations prior to the viva;
- what are vivas for? why have them?
- the build up to the viva;
- should your supervisor be there: pros and cons;
- what goes on in the viva: content and conduct;
- what might be asked in the viva examination – some safe bets;
- how students, with supervisors, can prepare and be prepared for the viva;
- the possible outcomes of a viva and how to deal with them.

Students' feelings, anticipations and expectations prior to the viva

The oral examination by viva voce (live voice) is of critical importance for students and their supervisors. It is an occasion where important decisions are made on your work so far – and it can also be an important event for shaping the future. We look at these purposes of the viva later in the chapter. First though, we focus on the emotional aspects of the process. Many doctoral students, especially those who are undertaking a professional doctorate, will be experienced at presenting orally during their own working lives. But presenting in the viva situation is likely to be a new experience and to offer a new challenge. For every doctoral candidate the viva is an important matter. For some it is a cause of anxiety and concern. For everyone involved, including the supervisor and sometimes the examiners, it is an emotional occasion.

From 2002 to 2009 I conducted 15 focus groups with doctoral students from a range of disciplines. The framework was simple: first I asked them to reflect upon and discuss with the person next to them their ***positive*** anticipations and feelings as they 'look forward' to the viva examination; these views were then 'collected' and presented to the group. Secondly, they were asked to do the same with their ***negative*** feelings and attitudes, followed by the same process of sharing and discussion. I do not have the space here to report in full on these focus groups as I have an archive of several hundred responses. However, I have categorised them into different groups, as shown below.

Positive anticipations

1   Feelings of the end, the climax – the start of a new life

Many students talked about the viva being the conclusion or their goal, using clichés such as the end, the climax, relief, closure, the final hurdle or the end product, with comments such as:

> It will be over and I can get on with my life.

> It's a climax ... a culmination of a long period of time.

> It's the end of PhD life – the aftermath begins.

2   A unique opportunity for feedback, improvement and dialogue with 'experts'

The second group of comments tends to relate to the unique, formative opportunity that the viva affords, and the anticipation that they will meet interested experts, specialists or new critics:

> I want to learn from it – I want it to be a quality experience.

> An opportunity to discuss and share your work with two new people – to have a dialogue with two experts.

> It will help to improve my thesis [commonly stated]; it will lead to improvement as a result of comments.

3   An event of legitimation and acceptance

A prevalent feeling is that the event will be a form of proof, of acceptance, of approval, of admittance and achievement, for example:

It gives legitimacy, value and credit to my work.

It will raise me up a level.

It gives status to our work.

It adds rigour.

I can gauge the level of my work.

4   An opportunity for clarification, explanation and defence

Many look forward to the event as a platform: a chance to talk, explain, defend, justify and contribute:

It is a chance to improve clarity and understanding.

I can consolidate and articulate my work.

5   A chance to show emotion and enthusiasm

The emotional aspect of the event comes through strongly with all students, both in their language and their behaviour or body language during these sessions. Comments included:

I can bring my thesis to life.

You can show your enthusiasm for what you've done.

It's a chance to shine.

I'm proud of my study and passionate about defending it before a panel [*sic*].

6   Anticipations of utility and future development

It might help me to get a job in academia.

It could open doors.

It could help me build my career and my publications through contact with the external examiner.

It could lead to publishing parts of it in a journal or book.

7   Feelings of confidence

In this seventh category of comment students talked of being able to show off, to clarify and explain, to show their strengths and the significance of what they have done. A surprising ebullience showed through in some comments:

You will know as much about the area as the examiners do.

I'll be centre stage.

You are presenting what you, yourself, have written; therefore it is what you know.

You can prove how good you are.

Nobody knows as much as you do about the topic.

You get to sell your ideas to others and show what you have achieved.

8   A chance to reflect, tell the story and consolidate

Finally, students talked of the reflective opportunity that the viva presents:

I can look back and remind myself of my PhD journey.

It is a chance to tell the whole story about the whole thesis (not just parts of it as you might do in an article) ... enthusiastically!

Negative anticipations and feelings

The next element of the focus groups involved reflecting on, sharing and discussing students' negative feelings in anticipating the viva. Again, a huge range of views and attitudes was collected, which I have attempted to classify into groups, using a selection of verbatim comments as illustrators:

1   Fears about the outcomes

I might fail.

Having to rewrite.

I will get feedback on my thesis – but will it be too late?

2   Worries about themselves before or during the viva

This tends to be by far the largest category of negative anticipation, with worries about not thinking straight, becoming too defensive, stage fright, talking too much, being too emotional, too tired or too stressed:

Will I be ineloquent?

I will be on the spot.

I may have moved on since I wrote my thesis.

Will my own personality come across badly, e.g. as being too aggressive?

You might not be able to respond to the questions even if you know the answers.

My mind might go blank and I'll want to leave the room.

It's a lot of brainwork compressed into a short time – quite a workload.

In addition, some overseas students talked of their fear of language barriers in the viva context.

3   Apprehensions relating to the examiners, their questions and their comments
Fears about the examiners, their agendas and their power struggles (perhaps spread by some of the horror stories that abound in electronic and non-electronic grapevines) form a large category:

> I'm afraid that some examiners will expect too much.
>
> Will I be questioned about areas that are marginal to or peripheral to my thesis?
>
> Examiners may have their own agendas.
>
> You don't know the exact questions that you will be made to answer.
>
> The examiners' interests and approaches may be different to yours.

Many students talked of being exposed, being asked questions they do not understand or having a completely unsympathetic examiner.

4   Anxieties about post-viva feelings
Finally, a minority talked of their worries about what follows after the viva and 'emptiness once it's finished', with comments such as:

> Where do I go from here?

In summary, students have a range of views, feelings and anticipations before their viva, as the comments above show clearly. They are all worth reflecting upon and sharing with fellow students; you might also wish to consider and explore them with your supervisor before the viva.

The purposes of the viva

What is the viva is actually for? Written regulations from universities should state the purpose of the viva. Common statements include: to test the candidate's knowledge of his/her research and subject area; to allow examiners to clarify any queries that may have arisen when reading the thesis; to judge whether the candidate has developed research skills appropriate to doctoral level; to give the candidate the opportunity to defend the thesis in person; to establish whether candidates fully understand the implications of their work. Some university regulations state explicitly that one of the main purposes is to ascertain whether the work is the candidate's own.

Many regulations quite rightly emphasise that the viva is an integral part of the examination of a postgraduate degree – in other words, the viva is actually part of the examining process, not (say) a confirmation of any pre-determined judgement. It is not a rubber-stamping exercise. Students and supervisors need to remind themselves of this – the examination as a whole involves more than just a judgement of the written work, i.e. the written and oral elements of the examination for a doctorate complement each other. For many universities, the written thesis is only part fulfilment of the requirements for a doctorate.

From a more negative perspective, if a thesis does not meet the necessary criteria, some university regulations state that one purpose of the viva is to ascertain reasons why a student's work is **not deemed to** attain doctoral standard. This might lead to questions about supervision, research training, resources or any mitigating personal circumstances.

What actually happens in the build up to a viva?

The oral examination or viva should be arranged within a set time period after the examiners receive your thesis. You might have to wait as long as 10 or even 12 weeks – you should check regulations for this. The organisation of the viva does not involve the student of course – depending on the university regulations, either the internal examiner, the independent chair (if the university uses this procedure) or the supervisor will have responsibility for arranging the date of the viva with the external examiner – this date should then be confirmed with the student, at the very least two weeks prior to the suggested date. A suitable venue is arranged, usually on the campus of the awarding university.

Both examiners usually complete a preliminary report on the thesis independently and then arrange to discuss your work before the viva. This meeting should be used to exchange and discuss their preliminary reports. (These reports are not seen in advance by the student or supervisor; however students can request to see them after the viva.) The two examiners should also decide on the procedure and content of the viva, i.e. what will be asked, who will be asking what and in what order. A good viva should have some sort of structure with prearranged questions and issues and a predetermined order. However, a viva should be viewed rather like a semi-structured interview – the discussion, if it is a good one, may lead on to other questions and sub-questions and may deviate from the plan.

In some universities, the external examiner is expected and invited to chair the viva. However, it is still the internal examiner's responsibility to check that procedures are followed correctly.

Can your supervisor come in? Should your supervisor come in?

In some cases (described as 'exceptional' in some university regulations) the supervisor may be present at the viva – but he or she should certainly not play a part in the actual discussion. My own view is that the student should confer with the supervisor on this issue and make the request between them.

There is a debate about the pros and cons of having one's supervisor present in the viva. Should your supervisor be present? On the plus side, you might feel that the supervisor's presence could give you support and confidence. A supervisor's presence may also be valuable when it comes to making notes, especially if revisions are ultimately required. (However, even if your supervisor is not present during the viva itself, he or she should be invited into the meeting after the viva to receive feedback and suggestions for amendment and the supervisor's job is then to take detailed notes on your behalf.) On the minus side, you might feel that the supervisor could be a distraction or an impediment to a full discussion. In all cases, if the supervisor is present, eye contact between student and supervisor seems best avoided (a suitable arrangement of chairs could ensure this).

What have students said to me when I have discussed this important issue with them? Students often present arguments in favour along the lines of: it can ensure fairness; the supervisor can take notes and feed back; it may help my nerves to see a familiar face and give me moral support; it will give me confidence and encouragement. Arguments against include: 'her or his presence may be a distraction'; 'it may be offputting'; 'I may not have had a good relationship with him or her'; 'it will make me even more nervous'; 'it could be embarrassing for me and for them'; 'I would rather like my supervisor *not* to be there as he does go to great lengths to clarify things!'; 'NO – it's an opportunity for me to discuss in depth the issues with my external examiner without my supervisor having pre-conceptions and putting forward their own views'. Many commented that the supervisor should certainly be on hand in case needed and that it should be the student's choice: 'It depends on your relationship!'

In summary, the presence or not of your supervisor is something you should discuss fully before the viva. Whether or not your supervisor is actually there during the viva itself, it is absolutely essential that he or she should be 'around' on the day of the viva. He or she should be invited into the viva room after the examination to be with you while you receive feedback on the outcomes of the viva (we look at these in a later section).

Content and conduct in the viva

The content of a viva examination will inevitably vary from one thesis to another, one field to another and between disciplines. However, there are certain general procedures for 'good practice' that are likely to be followed and indeed many university regulations insist that they are followed. We outline some of these first. Later, we list questions that we know have been, and still are, actually used in vivas.

Good practice

Students should expect certain aspects of good practice to be followed for the viva, although reality may fall short in some respects. The responsibility for ensuring good practice should fall on both the internal and external examiners. The venue for the viva may be someone's office or it could be in a seminar or meetings room. The room for the viva should be suitably laid out with seating organised so that eye contact can be made between student and examiners (if the supervisor is present, he or she should literally take 'a back seat'). The viva should start with polite introductions all round, led by the external examiner if he or she is the chair. The chair should explain what the viva is for, i.e. a focused discussion (not an interrogation) with others who know the field which gives the student a chance to defend the thesis. Most regulations do not permit examiners to tell students whether they have passed or failed at the start of the viva – this seems perfectly logical given that the viva is an integral part of the examination. No specific recommendations (regarding pass, fail, minor amendments, resubmission) should be made at all during the course of the viva; they must be conveyed clearly to student and supervisor after the examiners have conferred following the end of the viva. However, it seems civilised and conducive to a good discussion, to put the student at ease with a comment such as 'we have enjoyed reading your thesis, we found it very interesting and it raises some important issues'.

For most candidates, this will be their first viva (and possibly the last) so examiners should explain the process and procedures to them (in brief) – again with the aim of making them less nervous. It would seem to be good practice to start with a relatively easy, warm-up question: 'Tell us in brief what your thesis is about.' 'Why did you choose this topic to research?' 'What surprised you most in doing this study?' Specific questions will then follow, not all of which should have been pre-planned. The list which follows is based on my own experience of vivas both as an internal and external examiner over a period of 25 years of examining, though they will probably not be asked in this order.

Questions that might be asked in a viva for a doctorate

General
Motivation. What made you do this piece of research? Why did you choose this topic? Why do think it is important?

Position. What is your own position (professional or personal) in relation to this field and these research questions? What prior conceptions and/or experiences did you bring to this study? How did your own position/background/bias affect your data analysis and your data collection?

Contribution. Please could you summarise your thesis? What are the main findings of your research? What would somebody from this field learn from reading your thesis that they didn't know before? What did you learn from doing it? What original contribution to knowledge do you feel that you have made?

Publication. Which elements of your work do you feel are worthy of publication and/or presentation at a conference? What plans do you have for publication and dissemination? Has any of the work been published or presented already? (Note that the practice of disseminating some of the work via (say) a conference presentation or a journal paper is within the regulations of most universities – check your regulations on this.)

Theories and theoretical frameworks

Please talk us through the main research questions that you were trying to address in your work. What was the origin of these questions?

What theories/theoretical frameworks/perspectives have you drawn upon in your research?

Which theories did your study illuminate, if any?

Literature review

What shaped or guided your literature review? Why did it cover the areas that it did (and not others)? Why did you/didn't you include the work of X in your study?

On methodology and analysis of data

Methodology. Why did you employ the methods you used? Why not others, e.g. X? What informed your choice of methods? What would you do differently, with hindsight? What ethical issues did your study raise? How did you deal with them?

The sample. Why did you select this sample? Can you see any problems with it? If it is a small-scale study, can you justify why so few were involved? (Note that these questions would only apply with certain types of research.)

Data analysis: Did anything surprise you in the data ('hit you in the face')? Any anomalies? How did you analyse your data? How did you categorise/filter the data? Did themes emerge from your data (a posteriori) or did you 'bring them to the data' (a priori)? Why did you analyse it in this way? Could it have been done in another way?

Further work. Which aspects of the work could be taken further? How?

Generalisability and key messages

How far do think you can generalise from your work? What lessons can be learnt from it by practitioners/policy makers/other researchers? What are its key messages and implications?

Open forum

Reflections on the thesis. What are its strengths? And its limitations or weaknesses (with hindsight)? Is there anything else you would like to say or discuss that we have not asked you about?

Good practice in asking questions

Some university regulations actually give general guidance on good practice in asking questions. The University of Newcastle Handbook for Examiners of Research Degrees (2001) is particularly helpful here. The bullet points below are adapted from that handbook (pp. 7–8). Examiners should:

- ask questions in a constructive and positive way, as opposed to negative and confrontational, e.g. 'why did you use method X?' as opposed to 'why on earth did you decide to do Y?';
- use a range of questioning techniques, i.e. closed and open, specific and general;
- allow candidates time to reflect and to answer and encourage them to do this, i.e. not to rush but to take time and reflect before answering;
- praise good answers, e.g. if they are insightful, incisive or really help to clarify an issue or argument in the thesis;
- give candidates the opportunity to recover from a poor answer that may be a result of nerves or misunderstanding. Examiners may rephrase a question and pose it in a different way, thus helping not only to clarify it but also to allow the student some recovery time.

Some of these points are particularly important when English is an additional language for you as the student. The student may be far more at home with written English than with spoken English. It is the examiners' responsibility to speak clearly, to pose questions that are brief, clear and actually make sense, and to give students time to answer; indeed, this is good practice whatever the student's first language.

Your university department, especially if it has strong experience of selecting examiners, will usually have good knowledge of whom to avoid and whom to choose. You and your supervisor should draw upon this experience in choosing examiners, as we discussed in Chapter 8. The other important decision for a department is to select the right combination of internal and external examiner. There can sometimes be power struggles in this relationship – one should not dominate the other; they should be seen as equal partners in the process, whatever their status. Ideally, an external examiner should be chosen who knows the field, will explore all aspects of the thesis fully and will engage the candidate in a fair and demanding discussion but will not intimidate, confront or attempt to impress those present (including the internal examiner).

As a result, the viva should be a positive yet demanding experience.

Working with your supervisor in preparing for the viva

From the discussions earlier about the viva, its conduct and its perceived purposes it can be concluded that the key variables affecting the nature of a student's oral examination are likely to be:

- the written thesis itself;
- the regulations of the awarding university;
- the examiners: their views on the thesis, whether they have read and will follow regulations, their personal agendas and the likely chemistry or interpersonal interactions between them and between the student and the examiners.

The first two are relatively clear, at least in the sense that they are written documents in a way in the public domain. However, the manner in which they have been read and interpreted, alongside the variability in examiners and their personal characteristics, are certainly not clear and are undoubtedly difficult to predict. For those reasons it can be said that every viva is different – however, that is not a logical justification for not preparing for a viva. Preparation is vital. From my own experience, and from a reading of the literature in this area, I would make several general suggestions as a means of preparing for a viva:

- Know your thesis inside out.
- Have a mock viva, more to practise general oral skills, i.e. the ability to talk about the thesis and respond to challenges, than to attempt to predict specific questions or to rehearse stock answers.
- Talk to a range of others who have experienced vivas recently, but avoid horror stories.

- Be prepared to be criticised and challenged.
- Be prepared to defend your thesis and argue the case for what you have written.
- Be prepared to be asked to make (at the very least) minor amendments and possibly more fundamental changes to the written thesis.

This is probably the best general advice that can be given. On a more specific level, it is worth considering the list of possible questions above. It is very likely that at least some of them will be asked!

Murray (2003) gives useful practical advice on 'how to survive the viva', arguing that students should not simply accept the viva as something with 'mystique' and just wait to see what happens. She suggests a range of don'ts that include: don't be defensive, do not get angry, don't throw questions back at examiners and don't show reluctance to engage in debate. Murray also gives a range of ideas for preparing for the viva: practise answering difficult questions, including the 'two-minute answer'; practise the oral skills with different people, such as fellow students and colleagues; 'highlight the highlights' in the thesis and commit these to memory. These are all things that students can work on with their supervisor.

Finally, having been present in many vivas myself (as examiner or supervisor) it is worth saying that the types of question posed in the viva should be very similar to the questions that the supervisor is asking you at each supervisory meeting, right from day one. In both situations the questions will be about eliciting, clarifying, justifying, defending and explaining as in: Why did you do this and not this? What does this sentence mean? What have you done here? What are you planning to do here? In a sense, every supervisory meeting is a build up to the eventual viva (Trafford and Leshem, 2008).

Giving answers: the 'oral thesis'

By preparing for the viva, students can actually improve the quality of their answers. Students can then communicate and convey their thesis orally as well as in writing.

The written thesis should act as the foundation and source of your oral answers (Murray, 2003: 89) so you should have it to hand and look for your answers 'therein'. But good answers can clarify and extend points made in writing and can therefore often reduce the requirement for amendments after the viva. Equally, however, our experience is that in some viva situations students actually explain things or express things more clearly than they did in writing – furthermore, they may even add or extend new important points, arguments or messages that did not appear fully in writing at all.

This is perhaps one of the ironies in a good viva performance – the oral communication may extend and enhance the written thesis and therefore lead to a request that this enrichment be added to the written thesis.

Preparing for the viva, and of course writing the thesis, means learning the language. As Murray (2003: 90) puts it, you should be able 'to speak the language of your discipline fluently'. As with any language acquisition, this needs prior practice. It involves learning the key terms in your field and being able to define and explain them. If you are using words like epistemology, ontology, constructivism or paradigm, then be prepared to explain them. Don't throw them in (via writing or in speech) if you cannot explain their meaning in your context. Equally, the best and most testing way to find out if someone really knows the meaning of an abstract term or an item of jargon is to ask them to give concrete examples, illustrations or instances. Be prepared for this.

Another useful tip is to be specific when answering, partly (as Murray, 2003: 92 puts it) to 'show off'. If you mention an item of literature, give the detailed reference, right down to the author, date and page, if you can.

In answering the inevitable question about your 'original contribution', be upbeat without being arrogant. Rather than claiming world shattering originality or paradigm revolution you might lay claim to a fresh approach, a new perspective, different interpretation, modified theory or alternative model.

You will probably need to answer a call to reflect on the strengths and weaknesses in your work. Reflecting on its strengths will require some sort of claim for originality, as discussed above. I would suggest looking at weaknesses in terms of *limitations*. Everyone's work is limited in some way, even (perhaps especially in some circumstances) well-funded research. All researchers are limited in some way by time, resources, access to research sites and other constraining factors. Also, real-life research is messy and unpredictable – it is often the art of the possible. We suggest that students reflect on the limitations well in advance of the viva (including, of course, a section in the written thesis) and then present them in the viva in a positive light. For example, the need to **focus** on certain aspects of the literature or certain sites for data collection imposes limits. Difficult decisions have to be made in planning research and these lead to limitations and focus. The additional point to make in reflecting on the limits of your own work is that it points clearly to areas and imperatives for further research – and these pointers should be one of the strengths of your own thesis.

Finally, you should be asked whether there are any further points you would like to make that you have not expressed fully thus far in the viva. Be prepared for this, even if you feel that you do not need to speak further in your defence. You may be asked if you would like to pose any questions to the examiners. Again, be prepared for this. You might, if the viva has gone well, ask for ideas or possible outlets for publication of your research.

Table 10.1   Dos and don'ts before and during the viva

Don't	Do
Be dogmatic	Be thoughtful and reflective
Be defensive	Be honest
Be rude	Direct, but not rude
Be long winded	Be concise (but don't give one-word answers)
Try to please examiners by contriving to include their work in the references	Carry out some 'homework' on the examiners and their work
Demand certain examiners, e.g. for being the 'expert' in your field	Have some involvement in discussing and choosing the examiners
Be 'laid back' and blasé	Be prepared, but not over-prepared, e.g. by trying to predict questions
Be apologetic for what you've done	Be confident (but not over-confident)

By way of summary, Table 10.1 spells out some dos and don'ts that might be helpful in preparing for, and conducting yourself in, the viva examination.

Outcomes and action

Each institution will have some variations in the written regulations, but the outcomes are likely to fall into one of the following categories.

Pass
This is the unusual outcome when a thesis is accepted exactly as it stands, without any need for minor changes or corrections to typos. It is unlikely that a dissertation of tens of thousands of words contains no typographical errors, but this is what student and supervisor should aim for!

Minor amendments (sometimes called minor corrections or minor revision)
The thesis is passed, subject to minor amendments. The nature and extent of these can vary – from small alterations and correction of typing errors to making small revisions to sentences or paragraphs without major changes in the underlying thesis or the substance of the work. Examiners may also specify a *small* quantity of additional material to be added, e.g. a strengthening or a more explicit statement of the key messages perhaps, or suggestions for further research. There is often a fine line between this recommendation and the next. Many universities give a time limit of one month or 30 days (maximum) for this and indeed some may define the category of minor amendments as those that can realistically be done in a month. Some universities allow a maximum of three months. Usually, they require no further research by the candidate. Often, the changes will need to be approved only by the internal examiner.

Resubmission (sometimes called major corrections, major revision or referral)

Again, this can vary enormously from relatively minor amounts of rewriting, e.g. additions or amendments to the concluding chapter, to fairly major requests such as changing the data analysis and discussion. In some cases, the examiners may ask the student to go out and collect further data – and to do further analysis of the new data. In this category, some universities may ask for a more detailed literature review or an improved theoretical framing for the study. The maximum time allowed for a resubmission is usually one year.

Students can be asked to resubmit without the need for a further viva, provided the revised thesis is seen and approved by (in most cases) both examiners. In exceptional cases, when the viva has been very unsatisfactory, the recommendation may be for a resubmission followed by another viva. Finally, there may be a requirement for the candidate to undergo another viva examination without modification of the form or content of the written thesis, though this too is unusual.

Fail

This is a very uncommon decision and should not occur if the thesis has been carefully supervised and the student has taken and followed advice.

Approval for MPhil status

Again, this is unlikely in my experience, but it has happened. The doctorate is not awarded but the examiners recommend that the thesis be accepted at masters level, subject only to necessary changes to the title and cover.

These are generally the four or five categories of outcome which will be recommended by the examiners and which you and your supervisor will then need to take action on. Some universities use intermediate categories between minor amendments and resubmission such as 'limited corrections of an academic nature' (UEA, three months) and 'correction of modest errors or omissions' (Southampton, six months maximum). As an external examiner at Cambridge I was asked to decide between either 'minor or straightforward corrections' (to be done 'immediately after the viva') and 'more substantial or less straightforward amendments' (three months maximum).

Generally speaking, the most likely outcome is 'pass subject to revisions' in some form or other depending on the exact regulations. Following a viva, most students are asked to wait outside (hopefully in the supervisor's room rather than a corridor) so that examiners can reach an agreed decision. This may take some time, especially if the examiners cannot immediately reach a consensus. It is very often a case of needing to debate whether the thesis requires minor amendments or should be classed as needing a resubmission.

For students

When the feedback and the decision are given, I strongly advise that your supervisor is present (even if she/he was not there during the viva). If amendments are asked for, students should take great care to be crystal clear about the points being made and to clarify exactly what they need to do and to write. The heat of the moment, with the adrenaline flowing, is not always conducive to being able to understand, absorb and remember advice and feedback being given to you. Thus it is advisable to take notes yourself, but be sure to ask your supervisor to take notes and request the examiners to put their suggestions for amendment in writing. (This should be their duty anyway, according to most regulations.) If you are not clear, ask for clarification on the action you are being asked to take.

For supervisors

Making the necessary amendments, be they major, modest or minor, is a process which requires as much guidance and supervision as the production of the thesis prior to the viva. It is vitally important. It is not something which a student should be expected to do on his or her own. Rather like the initial completion of the thesis for the viva, it may well involve drafting and redrafting, seeking feedback and acting upon it, and having it finally checked by one's supervisor and another person or persons if possible. It is very much the last, but perhaps the most important phase of the supervision process.

In conclusion ...

One of the key messages of this chapter on the viva is that students should work closely with their supervisor(s) to make themselves ready for it – both parties should treat it as something that can be researched and prepared for. Practice does vary across institutions, so your own written regulations should be examined carefully; certain questions do recur, so it is worth preparing for the more general, commonly asked questions; there are guidelines and there is some consensus on 'good practice' for the viva, but not all of these will be followed all of the time. Doing a doctorate requires a high level of written skill and academic literacy – but succeeding in a viva requires an equal level of oral ability and academic oracy. Both need to be practised and prepared for – either in seminar sessions, conference presentations or mock vivas. The viva is an integral part of a doctoral examination, not an add-on or a rubber-stamping exercise. As Chapters 9 and 10 have stressed, there are two elements to a doctoral thesis: the written and the spoken.

The viva and the written thesis are important ways of presenting your doctoral work and making them public, especially once the thesis is housed and catalogued in the university library. In the final chapter of the book we present and discuss ways of disseminating your work more widely.

 Further reading

Denicolo, P. (2003) 'Assessing the PhD: a constructive view of criteria', *Quality Assurance in Education*, 11 (2): 84–91.

Murray, R. (2003) *How to Survive Your Viva*. Maidenhead: Open University Press.

Park, C. (2003) 'Levelling the playing field: towards best practice in the doctoral viva', *Higher Education Review*, 36 (1): 22–44.

Tinkler, P. and Jackson, C. (2004) *The Doctoral Examination Process*. Maidenhead: SRHE/Open University Press.

Trafford, V. and Leshem, S. (2008) *Stepping Stones to Achieving Your Doctorate: By Focusing on Your Viva from the Start*. Maidenhead: Open University Press.

11

After the viva:
recovering, publishing
and disseminating

 Chapter aims

This chapter considers:

- starting a new life? a new role for your supervisor?
- disseminating your work: the main possibilities;
- why publish ... and what puts people off?
- how can your supervisor help?
- getting published: ground rules and guidelines for journal articles;
- aiming for the book?

The after life

What should you do with your thesis after having your (probably) first and (hopefully) last ever viva? For many students, there can be a feeling of anticlimax after finishing their thesis and submitting it. I have even heard it being compared to post-natal depression. This can be felt even more deeply after the viva is over and any necessary rewriting has been completed. One possible antidote to this is to consider producing either one or more conference papers or journal articles from it, or possibly a book with a commercial publisher – after all, two of the key criteria for the award of a doctorate are that it should make a contribution to knowledge in an area and that at least some of it should be publishable.

This may well involve a new role for your supervisor – to some extent, helping students to 'get published' after the viva may be seen as somewhat beyond the call of duty; however, some universities go as far as to state that one of the supervisor's responsibilities is to 'encourage the publication of material contained in a successful thesis' (Loughborough University, *Notes for the Guidance of Research Students, Supervisors and Examiners,* 2006). This encouragement may occur after the viva or it may be part of the supervision process prior to the oral exam.

Disseminating: before, during or after?

One of the dilemmas that students face is whether to present, disseminate or publish any of their work *before* the doctoral thesis has been submitted. There are no hard and fast rules on this. As a supervisor, internal and external examiner I have seen many doctoral students present and publish aspects of their work (occasionally co-authored with their supervisor, which raises other issues) before the thesis has been examined. There is a range of possibilities for disseminating and presenting work in progress or work completed: some will involve spoken presentations, probably using visual aids; some will involve writing for conference proceedings, journals or book publishers; dissemination may involve a combination of spoken and written forms. Table 11.1 gives a summary of the main types of publication that could emerge from a research study.

Most doctoral students will and should be encouraged to present their work internally, for example at departmental seminars or an internally organised conference. Presenting to your peers can be a valuable experience for both presenter and audience. Another forum is the workshop or presentation session at a research association conference. A third audience is fellow practitioners, certainly for the researching professional. All or any of these modes of presentation can be used either during or after your doctoral programme, i.e. to present work in progress or work completed.

My own experience of students publishing in a written form (e.g. journal article or book chapter) before submission of the thesis is that this has not presented a problem for examiners, but I strongly suggest to students that they discuss this carefully with their supervisor before going ahead. Provided the writing of the article/paper is seen as an aid or a complement to writing the thesis, then it can be beneficial to a doctoral student to mould their work for a journal before the thesis is submitted. It can also be a valuable way of receiving (free!) feedback on one's work, either from referees or from participants at a conference, depending on the mode of publication.

Table 11.1   Main types of research publication

Articles ('papers') in peer-reviewed journals	With respect to their content, papers can be divided into: • *primary literature* – reports of new, previously unpublished data; • *narrative literature reviews* – critical summaries of a current state of knowledge on a given topic; • *quantitative literature reviews/metaanalyses* – 'pulling together' and statistical reanalysis of results of all (quantitative) studies on one particular topic, in order to draw a general conclusion about their outcome.
Books	With respect to authorship and the editorial process, academic books may be divided into: • *scholarly monographs* – books addressing a single topic, written by one or few authors; • *edited books* – books where each chapter is written by different authors. Chapters are revised by editors who take responsibility for overall consistency, coherence and cohesion. They usually (though not exclusively) address a single topic. With respect to content, academic books are typically narrative literature reviews, though they may also report primary findings or quantitative literature review/metanalyses.
Presentations at conferences (organised by learned societies or professional organisations)	Different forms are possible: • *oral presentations* – oral accounts (typically using visual aids) of research in front of the peer audience; • *posters* – a 'single page' summary of research, presented during 'poster sessions' that are part of most conferences; • *conference proceedings* – printed summaries of research presented during conferences. May be very brief (abstracts) or more substantial (resembling research papers).
Commissioned scientific reports	The commissioning body may be the government, a charity, a quango, a commercial company, etc.
Other	• *Technical reports* – typically prepared for internal distribution (e.g. for a sponsor of the research project). • *Working papers* – reports of work in progress, ahead of more formal peer-reviewed publication. They are often made available online. • *Blogs* – blogs as the means of disseminating research findings have been increasingly adopted, e.g. by some scientists researching online communities.

Adapted from Wellington and Szczerbinski (2007).

Why publish ... and what puts people off?

One of the first things to discuss, with both your peers and your supervisor, is the question: why publish? This is the starting point because it will determine not only which parts of your study you might aim to disseminate more widely but also which targets you should aim for (e.g. journal or book? which types of journal? book chapters?) and whom you should work with in achieving these goals.

Over a number of years I have been asked to run seminars for students and new lecturers on publishing. I always begin with the question: what are your motives for wanting to publish? The responses are many and varied (several have been recorded in more detail in Wellington, 2003: 2–11). Quite commonly, the motivations are extrinsic: to improve my CV, to get a job, to gain promotion, to join the research community, to earn respect and credibility, to enhance my standing, to become known and so on. But equally commonly, the motivation for publishing is more an intrinsic one: to clarify my own thinking, to share my ideas more widely, for personal satisfaction, as a contribution to change and improvement, to make a difference, to set up a dialogue, and so on.

On the other side of the coin, I also explore with students and new lecturers some of the factors which prevent them from publishing or even attempting to do so. Responses are again many and varied but include such feelings as: lack of self-belief, fear of criticism or rejection, not knowing where to begin, wondering 'am I good enough?', not having a track record, lack of time and energy, not knowing the right targets and so on.

All of the above motivating *and* demotivating factors are important in considering how to proceed and, specifically, how to work with your supervisor. For example, if your aim is to gain a job or promotion within academia, then you should be consulting your supervisor about which targets for publications – probably academic journals – are most appropriate. On the other hand, if your work relates to a particular profession (most likely if you are doing a professional doctorate) then the motivation for publishing and the most productive 'outlet' for it will be different. When we consider demotivating factors then the role of the supervisor in guiding and assisting is equally important. If a student has no track record (a likely position) and lacks confidence or does not know where to begin then the collaboration and direct help of the supervisor is essential. Students may wish to co-author with their supervisor and this can often be the best way to get started. If someone wishes to go it alone, then the advice from supervisor(s) on content, critical reading and guidance on potential journal target or book publisher is vital. There may also be other staff in the department, whom the supervisor can help you liaise with, who may be editors of major journals or on editorial boards or (equally likely) will have good contacts with commissioning editors for book publishers.

My advice is to use all the networks and contacts that you can find when it comes to publishing and finding a target for your work. Your supervisor can play a central part in this as a facilitator, adviser, guide or co-author – or all of these roles.

Converting your thesis to a 'publication' ... or more

For many students, the last thing they feel like doing after the examination process is complete is to return to their thesis and start to chop it up and mould it into some other form or forms. But this is exactly what is required. Perhaps the best tactic is to ignore it for several weeks, putting some time and distance between you and it, and then to return to it with the explicit aim of disseminating your work and getting published. You may wish to be the sole author, which is fine, but the act of getting started is best done in collaboration with someone else, preferably your supervisor or a colleague who has experience of writing for journals or book publishers.

The first task is to set some goals. The thesis may contain different papers for different audiences. For example, there may be an important article to be written from the thesis on the methodology or even the specific methods used, or if a thesis has a very strong, critical, perhaps systematic review of the literature in one area then this may form the basis of a publishable article. These might be targeted (see later) on one journal. Another article might be written on the findings and their implications for practice – this might be geared at a more professional journal aimed at practitioners such as teachers or lecturers. Thirdly, within the thesis there might be an article that can contribute to thinking and theory within an area; and finally, between the two poles of practice and theory, there might be important messages for policy-makers and planners, and this might be targeted at a refereed journal on policy or a more professional journal for policy-makers. It may be that the external or internal examiner has been particularly complimentary about one or more sections of your thesis and these may be singled out for 'converting' into a publication for a journal.

If the goal is to be a book, then it might contain a combination of all the above. However, commercial book publishers will want a clear statement of the potential market for the book and this is discussed shortly.

Going for journal articles – strategies and tactics

There is not the space in this book to explore fully the intricacies of writing and refereeing for, or even editing, journals (for a fuller account see Wellington, 2003: chapter 4). All I can do here is sum up some of the key tips for new writers (Table 11.2) and indicate some of the things not to do (Table 11.3).

First, it is important that you should have a clear target journal in mind *before* you write your article, not after. This means that your first job is to

Table 11.2   Writing for journals: tips for improving acceptance chances

- Select a journal and familiarise yourself with it, i.e. select your target journal carefully and tailor your manuscript to suit it and its intended audience.
- Look for recurring topics, debates and themes.
- Decide on the type of journal and who it is for, i.e. wide ranging or specialist? Professional or academic? Refereed or non-refereed?
- Read a good number of back issues and shape your article accordingly.
- Look for traits/characteristics in a journal and attempt to model them.
- Try to make a unique contribution, however small.
- Try to write clearly and coherently.
- Have a clear argument or thesis running through it.
- Include a 'so what?' section.
- Keep to the word length.
- Follow the journal's guidelines to authors, especially on citation style and referencing.
- Observe how past authors have structured their writing.
- Check journal style and past practice on headings and subheadings.
- Ask a critical friend to read it before sending it off.

Table 11.3   Writing for journals: common mistakes

1   Lack of familiarity with the journal, its style and its readership.
2   Wrong style, wrong formatting, etc.
3   Wrong length.
4   Poor presentation, e.g. grammatical errors, typos.
5   No substance – 'much ado about nothing'.
6   Unreadability, i.e. writing is unclear, turgid or does not make sense.
7   Manuscript not checked and proofread.

become aware of all the possible journals in your field that are potential targets. (Incidentally, as we saw in Chapter 10, this may well be an area that you are questioned on in your viva.) You should also be aware of the following:

- There will be considerable time lags between submission and receiving referees' comments – and between acceptance and actual appearance in print (in the region of two years in some cases).
- Peer review can be difficult to accept, but you should view it positively, i.e. as free feedback and a way of making your article better.
- Do expect to have to make at least some revisions to your first submission.
- You may be rejected by one journal – if so, then improve your first version and send it to another journal as soon as possible.

The main message is that you should not be discouraged by letters that say you need to make changes (this is to be expected, not feared) – make the changes and that journal will often publish the revised version.

Finally, there is one definite **don't** with journal articles (incidentally, this is not as clear-cut with book proposals). It is now an accepted ethical code in most fields (a written code in some cases, tacit in others) that authors should never submit the same article to more than one journal concurrently, i.e. one should submit in series, not parallel, even though this takes time.

Going for the book?

Journal articles are written for peers, but books are written for markets. Different rules of engagement apply. Commercial publishers will not publish books that people are unlikely to buy. No commercial book publisher will ever accept a traditional thesis exactly as it stands and convert it straight into a book. (See Wellington, 2003: chapter 5, for evidence to support this trend.) The conversion is your job – but the task of converting a thesis into a book is no small one. It involves radical changes to the content, including much chopping down. It will need a new title, agreeable to the publisher. The audience and therefore the style of writing will be different. In short, it requires severe editing, extensive rewriting and certainly a large element of repackaging or remoulding.

No one should ever write a book before seeking and finding a publisher, having one's proposal scrutinised and advised upon, and then receiving a contract safely in hand. Book proposals require considerable thought partly because, unlike theses, books have to be sold, meaning that somebody must want to buy them. Usually, a proposal will consist of a synopsis of the book and one or two sample chapters. But what else should a typical proposal contain? There is a fair measure of agreement among different publishers on the sections that should be covered in a good book proposal. These are summarised in Table 11.4.

Table 11.4   The key elements in a book proposal

- The provisional title of the book.
- Its proposed contents: what will the book be about?
- A synopsis.
- The market, the intended readership: who is going to buy it?
- The competition: how will it compare with, compete with or complement existing books?
- Who is the author?
- The timescale and writing plan: when will the script be ready?
- Production requirements: how long will it be (the extent), how many tables, illustrations, etc. will it contain?
- Sample material: one, or at most two, draft chapters.
- Potential referees for this proposal.

If anyone would like full details and further insight, based on interviews with publishers, the business of writing a book proposal and publishers' criteria for acceptance are discussed at length in Wellington (2003: 81–95). In addition, most commercial publishers provide their own guidelines and pro forma.

My own experience with publishers and their commissioning editors is that they are extremely helpful and will often support a good idea even if it will not result in the sale of tens of thousands of books. However, one point is worth bearing in mind from a career point of view: authors who intend to go into academia after their doctorate will be subject to research assessment exercises – hence, they need to be conscious of steering the right course between audience appeal and scholarly substance. A book with popular appeal may not always carry the same kudos as an article in a high-status journal.

In conclusion ... entering the community of scholars

This chapter has discussed the important business of deciding what to do after your viva. Should you accept your degree, be content to see your thesis installed in the university library (or the electronic repository if it is also submitted as an e-thesis) and forget about it? Or should you continue to work with your supervisor and consider the pros and cons of publishing some or most of it in the form of articles, book chapters or even a book? We have examined the various ways of disseminating the work in a thesis, the motivations for putting in this extra effort and some of the reasons that put people off.

My suggestion is to go for it. For many established authors, their first academic book or journal article was a by-product of their masters or doctoral thesis; many theses have the potential to be transformed into a book, a book chapter or an article or more. The article or book is unlikely to have the extensive data presentation, tables of results, comprehensive literature review, methodology discussion, terms of conditionality, appendices and plethora of references that would be expected in a doctoral thesis – but its central themes, its original contribution to knowledge and its innovative ideas and discussion are all likely to interest a book publisher or a journal editor. Everyone starts somewhere. The viva and the written thesis are the first steps to getting known and entering the 'community of scholars' that people talk about but that newcomers often find difficult to locate and become a part of. Conference presentations and posters, papers and journal articles, and books all have a role in feeling part of that community.

Further reading

Day, A. (1996) *How to Get Research Published in Journals*. Aldershot: Gower Press.

Dinham, S. and Scott, C. (2001) 'The experience of disseminating the results of doctoral research', *Journal of Further and Higher Education*, 25 (1): 45–55.

Kitchin, R. and Fuller, D. (2005) *The Academic's Guide to Publishing*. London: Sage.

McCallum, C. (1997) *Writing for Publication*, 4th edn. Oxford: How To Books.

Wellington, J. (2003) *Getting Published*. London: Routledge.

References and further reading

Acker, S. (1999) 'Students and supervisors: the ambiguous relationship. Perspectives on the supervisory process in Britain and Canada', in A. Holbrook and S. Johnston (eds), *Supervision of Postgraduate Research in Education'*, *Review of Australian Research in Education*, 5: 75–94.

Ahem, K. and Manathunga, C. (2004) 'Clutch-starting stalled research students', *Innovative Higher Education*, 28 (4): 237–54.

Andrade, M. S. (2006) 'International students in English-speaking universities: adjustment factors', *Journal of Research in International Education*, 5 (2): 131–54.

Appadurai, A. (1990) 'Disjuncture and difference in the global cultural economy', *Public Culture*, 2 (2): 1–24.

Appel, L. and Dahlgren, L. (2003) 'Swedish doctoral students' experiences on their journey towards a PhD: obstacles and opportunities inside and outside the academic building', *Scandinavian Journal of Educational Research*, 47 (1): 89–110.

Beck, U. (2000) *What Is Globalisation?* Cambridge: Polity Press.

Becker, H. (1986) *Writing for Social Scientists*. Chicago: Chicago University Press.

Becker, L. (2004) 'Working with your supervisor', in *How to Manage Your Postgraduate Course*. London: Palgrave, chapter 5.

Bloom, B. A. (ed.) (1956) *Taxonomy of Educational Objections: The Classification of Educational Goals – Handbook I: Cognitive Domain*. New York: McKay.

Boice, R. (1997) 'Strategies for enhancing scholarly productivity', in J. M. Moxley and T. Taylor (eds), *Writing and Publishing for Academic Authors*. Lanham, MD: Rowman & Littlefield, pp. 19–34.

Boud, D. and Lee, A. (2005) '"Peer learning" as pedagogic discourse for research education', *Studies in Higher Education*, 30 (5): 501–16.

Bowen, W. G. and Rudenstein, N. L. (1992) *In Pursuit of the PhD*. Princeton, NJ: Princeton University Press.

Brande, D. (1983) *Becoming a Writer*. London: Macmillan.

Brause, R. S. (2000) *Writing Your Doctoral Dissertation: Invisible Rules for Success*. London: Falmer.

Brown, G. and Atkins, M. (1988) *Effective Teaching in Higher Education*. London: Methuen.

Burnett Report (1977) 'Report of the Vice-Chancellor's Committee on research and postgraduate study', cited in I. Moses (1984) 'Supervision of higher degree students – problem areas and possible solutions', *Higher Education Research and Development*, 3 (2): 153–65.

Burnham, P. (1994) 'Surviving the viva: unravelling the mysteries of the PhD oral', *Journal of Graduate Education*, 1 (1): 30–4.

Caffarella, R. S. and Bamet, E. G. (2000) 'Teaching doctoral students to become scholarly writers: the importance of giving and receiving critiques', *Studies in Higher Education*, 25 (1): 39–52.

Conrad, L. (1994) 'Gender and postgraduate supervision', in Y. Ryan and O. Zuber-Skerritt (eds), *Quality in Postgraduate Education*. London: Kogan Page: pp. 51–8.

Connell, R. (1985) 'How to supervise a PhD', *Vestes*, 2: 38–41.

Council of Graduate Schools (1991) *The Role and Nature of the Doctoral Dissertation*. Washington, DC: CGS.

Cribb, J. and Gewirtz, S. (2006) 'Doctoral student supervision in a managerial climate', *International Studies in the Sociology of Education*, 16 (3): 223–36.

Cryer, P. (2000) *The Research Student's Guide to Success*. Buckingham: Open University Press.

Davies, C. and Birbili, M. (2000) 'What do people need to know about writing in order to write in their jobs?', *British Journal of Educational Studies*, 48 (4): 429–45.

Day, A. (1996) *How to Get Research Published in Journals*. Aldershot: Gower Press.

Deem, R. (1998) '"New managerialism" and higher education: the management of performances and cultures in universities in the UK', *International Studies in Sociology of Education*, 8: 47–70.

Delamont, S., Atkinson, P. and Parry, O. (1998) 'Creating a delicate balance: the doctoral supervisor's dilemma', *Teaching in Higher Education*, 3 (2): 157–72.

Delamont, S., Atkinson, P. and Parry, O. (2000) *The Doctoral Experience: Success and Failure in Graduate School*. London: Palmer.

Delamont, S., Atkinson, P. and Parry, O. (2004) *Supervising the Doctorate*. Maidenhead: Open University Press.

Delton, J. (1985) *The 29 Most Common Writing Mistakes and How to Avoid Them*. Cincinnati, OH: Writer's Digest Books.

Denicolo, P. (2003) 'Assessing the PhD: a constructive view of criteria', *Quality in Education*, 11 (2): 84–91.

Denicolo, P. and Pope, M. (1994) 'The postgraduate's journey: interplay of roles', in O. Zuber-Skerritt and Y. Ryan (eds), *Quality in Postgraduate Education*. London: Kogan Page.

Dinham, S. and Scott, C. (2001) 'The experience of disseminating the results of doctoral research', *Journal of Further and Higher Education*, 25 (1): 45–55.

Duke, C. (1992) *The Learning University: Towards a New Paradigm*. Buckingham: SRHE/ Open University Press.

Economic and Social Research Council (ESRC) (1991) *Postgraduate Training: Guidelines on the Provision of Research Training for Postgraduate Research Students in the Social Sciences*. Swindon: ESRC.

Elbow, P. (1981) *Writing Without Teachers*. Oxford: Oxford University Press.

Eley, A. and Jennings, R. (2005) *Effective Postgraduate Supervision*. Maidenhead: Open University Press.

Enders, J. (2004) 'Research training and careers in transition: a European perspective on the many faces of the PhD', *Studies in Continuing Education*, 26 (3): 419–29.

Farrar, V. and Young, R. (2008) *Supervising Disabled Research Students*, Guides on Postgraduate Issues, New Series No 3. London: Society for Research into Higher Education.

Gatfield, T. (2005) 'An investigation into PhD supervisory management styles: development of a dynamic conceptual model and its managerial implications', *Journal of Higher Education Policy and Management*, 27 (3): 311–25.

Grabe, W. and Kaplan, R. (1996) *Theory and Practice of Writing*. New York: Longman.

Grant, B. (2005) 'Fighting for space in supervision: fantasies, fairytales, fictions and fallacies', *International Journal of Qualitative Studies in Education*, 18 (3): 337–54.

Green, H. and Powell, S. (2005) *Doctoral Study in Contemporary Higher Education*. Buckingham: Open University Press.

Green, P. and Usher, R. (2003) 'Fast supervision: changing supervisory practice', *Studies in Continuing Education*, 25 (1): 37–50.

Hartley, J. (1997) 'Writing the thesis', in N. Graves and V. Varma (eds), *Working for a Doctorate*. London: Routledge, pp. 96–112.

Hartley, J. and Jory, S. (2000) 'Lifting the veil on the viva: the experiences of psychology PhD candidates in the UK', *Psychology Teaching Review*, 9 (2): 76–90.

Hasrati, M. (2005) 'Legitimate peripheral participation and supervising PhD students', *Studies in Higher Education*, 30 (5): 557–70.

Haynes, A. (2001) *Writing Successful Textbooks*. London: A & C Black.

Henson, K. (1999) *Writing for Professional Publication*. Boston: Allyn & Bacon.

Higher Education Funding Council for England (2005) *PhD Research Degrees: Entry and Completion*. Bristol: Higher Education Funding Council for England.

Higher Education Funding Council for England (2007) *Research Degree Qualification Rates*. Bristol: Higher Education Funding Council for England.

Hill, T., Acker, S. and Black, E. (1994) 'Research students and their supervisors in education and psychology', in R. G. Burgess (ed.), *Postgraduate Education and Training in the Social Sciences*. London: Jessica Kingsley.

Hockey, J. (1997) 'A complex craft: UK PhD supervision in the social sciences', *Research in Post-Compulsory Education*, 2: 45–70.

Ivanic, R. (1998) *Writing and Identity: The Discoursal Construction of Identity in Academic Writing*. Amsterdam: John Benjamins.

Ives, G. and Rowley, G. (2005) 'Supervisor selection or allocation and continuity of supervision: PhD students' progress and outcomes', *Studies in Higher Education*, 30 (5): 535–55.

Jackson, C. and Tinkler, P. (2001) 'Back to basics: a consideration of the purposes of the PhD viva', *Assessment and Evaluation in Higher Education*, 26 (4): 355–66.

Johnson, L., Lee, A. and Green, B. (2000) 'The PhD and the autonomous self: gender, rationality, and postgraduate pedagogy', *Studies in Higher Education*, 25: 135–47.

Joyner, R. (2003) 'The selection of external examiners for research degrees', *Quality in Higher Education*, 11 (2): 123–7.

Kitchin, R. and Fuller, D. (2005) *The Academic's Guide to Publishing*. London: Sage.

Krause, E. (2007) '"Maybe the communication between us was not enough": inside a dysfunctional advisor/L2 advisee relationship', *English for Academic Purposes*, 6: 55–70.

Lave, J. and Wenger, E. (1991) *Situated Learning: Legitimate Peripheral Participation*. Cambridge: Cambridge University Press.

Lee, A. (2008) 'How are doctoral students supervised? Concepts of doctoral research and supervision', *Studies in Higher Education*, 33 (3): 267–81.

Lee, D. (1998) 'Sexual harassment in PhD supervision', *Gender and Education*, 10 (3): 299–312.

Leonard, D. (2001) *A Woman's Guide to Doctoral Studies*. Buckingham: Open University Press.

Leonard, D., Becker, R. and Coate, K. (2005) 'To prove myself at the highest level: the benefits of doctoral study', *Higher Education Research and Development*, 24 (2): 135–49.

Lewin, K. (1951) *Field Theory in Social Science: Selected Theoretical Papers*, ed. D. Cartwright. New York: Harper & Row.

Lillis, T. (2001) *Student Writing: Access, Regulation, Desire*. London: Routledge.

McAlpine, L. and Weiss, J. (2000) 'Mostly true confessions: joint meaning making about the thesis journey', *Canadian Journal of Higher Education*, 30 (1): 1–26.

McCallum, C. (1997) *Writing for Publication*, 4th edn. Oxford: How to Books.

McWilliam, E. and James, R. (2002) 'Doctoral education in a knowledge economy', *Higher Education Research and Development*, 21 (2): 117.

Malfoy, J. and Webb, C. (2000) 'Congruent and incongruent views of postgraduate supervision', in M. Kiley and G. Mullins (eds), *Quality in Postgraduate Research: Making Ends Meet*. Adelaide: Advisory Centre for University Education, University of Adelaide, pp. 155–77.

Manathunga, C. (2005) 'Early warning signs in postgraduate research education: a different approach to ensuring timely completions', *Teaching in Higher Education*, 10 (2): 219–33.

Medawar, P. (1963) 'Is the scientific paper a fraud?', *The Listener*, September.

Medawar, P. (1976) *Advice to a Young Scientist*. London: Harper & Row.

Morley, L. (2004) 'Interrogating doctoral assessment', *International Journal of Educational Research*, 41 (2): 91–7.

Morley, L., Leonard, D. and David, M. (2002) 'Variations in vivas: quality and equality in British PhD assessments', *Studies in Higher Education*, 27 (3): 263–73.

Moxley, J. (1997) 'If not now, when?', in J. Moxley and T. Taylor (eds), *Writing and Publishing for Academic Authors*. Lanham, MD: Rowman & Littlefield, pp. 6–19.

Mullins, G. and Kiley, M. (2002) 'It's a PhD, not a Nobel Prize: how experienced examiners assess research theses', *Studies in Higher Education*, 27 (4): 369–86.

Murray, R. (2002) *How to Write a Thesis*. Buckingham: Open University Press.

Murray, R. (2003) *How to Survive Your Viva*. Buckingham: Open University Press.

Neumann, D. (2007) 'Policy and practice in doctoral education', *Studies in Higher Education*, 32 (4): 459–73.

Neumann, R. (2003) *The Doctoral Education Experience: Diversity and Complexity*. Canberra: Australian Government, Department of Education, Science and Training. Online at: http://www.dest.gov.au/NR/rdonlyres/873B3698-F3BA-4D86-869C-OC3C6DB95658/804/Q3 12.pdf (accessed 10 June 2008).

Nyquist, J. D. and Woodford, B. J. (2000) *Re-envisioning the PhD: What Concerns Do We Have?* Washington, DC: University of Washington.

Park, C. (2003) 'Levelling the playing field: towards best practice in the doctoral viva', *Higher Education Review*, 36 (1): 22–44.

Park, C. (2007) *Redefining the Doctorate*. York: Higher Education Academy.

Parry, S. (2007) *Disciplines and Doctorates*. Dordrecht: Springer.

Pearce, L. (2005) *How to Examine a Thesis*. Buckingham: SRHE/Open University Press.

Pearson, M. and Brew, A. (2002) 'Research training and supervision development', *Studies in Higher Education*, 27 (2): 138–43.

Phillips, E. and Pugh, D. (1987) *How to Get a PhD*. Buckingham: Open University Press.

Phillips, E. and Pugh, D. (2000) *How to Get a PhD: A Handbook for Students and Their Supervisors*, 3rd edn. Buckingham: Open University Press.

Postlethwaite, K. (1993) *Differentiated Science Teaching*. Milton Keynes: Open University Press.

Powell, S. and Green, H. (2007) *The Doctorate World Wide*. Buckingham: Society for Research into Higher Education and Open University Press.

Quality Assurance Agency for Higher Education (QAA) (2004) *Code of Practice for the Assurance of Academic Quality and Standards in Higher Education*. Gloucester: QAA.

Richardson, L. (1990) *Writing Strategies: Reaching Diverse Audiences*. Newbury Park, CA: Sage.

Richardson, L. (1998) 'Writing: a method of inquiry', in N. Denzin and Y. Lincoln (eds), *Collecting and Interpreting Qualitative Materials*. London: Sage.

Richardson, L. (2000) 'Writing: a method of inquiry', in N. Denzin and Y. Lincoln (eds), *The Handbook of Qualitative Research*, 2nd edn. Thousand Oaks, CA: Sage.

Robson, S. and Turner, Y. (2007) '"Teaching is a co-learning experience": academics reflecting on learning and teaching in an "internationalized" faculty', *Teaching in Higher Education*, 12 (1): 41–54.

Rudd, E. (1985) *A New Look at Postgraduate Failure*. London: Society for Research into Higher Education and National Foundation for Educational Research.

Rudestam, K. and Newton, R. (1992) *Surviving Your Dissertation*. London: Sage.

Sadak, J. (2004) *Doctoral Studies and Qualifications in Europe and the United States*, UNESCO Studies in Higher Education. Online at: wwwxepes.ro/publications/pdf/doctorate.pdf.

Scott, D., Brown, A., Lunt, I. and Thorne, L. (2004) *Professional Doctorates: Integrating Professional and Academic Knowledge*. Maidenhead: SRHE/Open University Press.

Seagram, B. C., Gould, J. and Pyke, S. W. (1998) 'An investigation of gender and other variables on time to completion of doctoral degrees', *Review of Higher Education*, 39 (3): 319–35.

Sillitoe, J. and Crosling, G. (1999) 'Thesis planning and writing: a structured approach', in Y. Ryan and O. Zuber-Skerritt (eds), *Supervising Postgraduates from Non-English Speaking Backgrounds*. Buckingham: Open University Press.

Simpson, R. (1983) *How the PhD Came to Britain*. Guildford: Society for Research into Higher Education.

Smedley, C. (1993) *Getting Your Book Published*. Newbury Park, CA: Sage.

Sprent, P. (1995) *Getting into Print*. London: E.& F.N. Spon.

Taylor, S. and Beasley, N. (2005) *A Handbook for Doctoral Supervisors*. London: RoutledgeFalmer.

Thomas, G. (1987) 'The process of writing a scientific paper', in P. Hills (ed.), *Publish or Perish*. Ely: Peter Francis, pp. 93–117.

Tinkler, P. and Jackson, C. (2002) 'In the dark? Preparing for the PhD viva', *Quality Assurance in Education*, 10 (2): 86–97.

Tinkler, P. and Jackson, C. (2004) *The Doctoral Examination Process: A Handbook for Students, Examiners and Supervisors*. Maidenhead: SRHE/Open University Press.

Torrance, M. S. and Thomas, G. V. (1994) 'Postgraduate education and training in the social sciences', in R. G. Burgess (ed.), *Postgraduate Education and Training in the Social Sciences: Processes and Products*. London: Jessica Kingsley, pp. 105–23.

Trafford, V. and Leshem, S. (2008) *Stepping Stones to Achieving Your Doctorate: By Focusing on Your Viva from the Start*. Maidenhead: Open University Press.

Trice, A. (2005) 'Navigating in a multinational learning community: academic departments: responses to graduate international students', *Journal of Studies in International Education*, 9 (1): 62–89.

UKCGE (2002) *Professional Doctorates*. Staffordshire: UK Council for Graduate Education.

Usher, R. (2002) 'A diversity of doctorates: fitness for the knowledge economy?', *Higher Education Research and Development*, 21 (2): 143–53.

Wellington, J. (2000) *Educational Research: Contemporary Issues and Practical Approaches*. London and New York: Continuum.

Wellington, J. (2003) *Getting Published*. London: Routledge.

Wellington, J. (2006) *Secondary Education: The Key Concepts*. London: Routledge.

Wellington, J. and Ireson, G. (2008) *Science Teaching, Science Learning*. London: Routledge.

Wellington, J. and Sikes, P. (2006) '"A doctorate in a tight compartment": why do students choose a professional doctorate and what impact does it have on their personal and professional lives?', *Studies in Higher Education*, 31 (6): 723–34.

Wellington, J. and Szczerbinski, M. (2008) *Research Methods for the Social Sciences*. London: Continuum.

Wellington, J., Bathmaker, A., Hunt, C., McCulloch, G. and Sikes, P. (2005) *Succeeding with your Doctorate*. London: Sage.

Wenger, E. (1998) *Communities of Practice: Learning, Meaning, and Identity*. Cambridge: Cambridge University Press.

Wisker, G. (2001) *The Post Graduate Research Handbook*. London: Palgrave Macmillan.

Wisker, G., Robinson, G., Trafford, V., Creighton, E. and Warnes, M. (2003) 'Recognizing and overcoming dissonance in postgraduate student research', *Studies in Higher Education*, 28 (1): 91–105.

Wolcott, H. (1990) *Writing Up Qualitative Research*. Newbury Park, CA: Sage.

Woods, P. (1999) *Successful Writing for Qualitative Researchers*. London: Routledge.

Woodwark, J. (1992) *How to Run a Paper Mill: Writing Technical Papers and Getting Them Published*. Winchester: Information Geometers Ltd.

Zhao, F. (2003) 'Transforming quality in research supervision: a knowledge-management approach', *Quality in Higher Education*, 9 (2): 187–99.

Zinsser, W. (1983) *Writing with a Word Processor*. New York: Harper & Row.

Index